"Regardless of the crisis you are facing, you need this testimony. God can move any mountain. He can deliver you from any problem."

    Dr. Brian Disney, Senior Pastor
    Mission Boulevard Baptist Church, Fayetteville, Arkansas

"Sometimes God's answers to your prayers will surprise you. Dr. Briney never expected the answer to his prayer to be life threatening. But the Lord granted his prayer with a healing miracle."

    Jerry Locke, Retired Pastor and Author
    Lakeworth, Texas

"Pat was an incredible fighter during his illness. Although he fought through two bouts of Hodgkin's lymphoma, he never lost hope and never stopped praying! His battle with cancer didn't quench his desire to know God in a more intimate way. This book reveals how the impossible becomes possible through prayer!"

    Lepaine Sharp-McHenry, DNP, RN
    Dean and Professor, College of Natural, Behavioral, and Health Sciences, Simmons University

"Some things cannot be fixed but by prayer and a miracle. Dr. Briney's testimony will inspire you to pray and expect a miracle."

    P.D. Taylor, Pastor
    Pleasant Valley Baptist Church, Dallas, Texas

"HOPE and PRAY are two books that every believer will want to read. In HOPE, Dr. Briney shares how God answered his prayer to understand the prayers that move mountains. God gave him a mountain and then moved it. In PRAY, readers will discover how God answers every prayer and how to recognize every answer. These two books will change how you pray."

    Travis Jones, Pastor
    Highland Baptist Church, El Reno, Oklahoma

"Want to know how to access God's infinite resources and find out how to recognize God's answers to every one of your prayers? Read this book!"

> Darrell W. Sparks, Pastor
> Dearborn Baptist Church, Aurora, Indiana

"Dr. Briney's personal testimony of God's healing power will enlighten every reader with insights into what prayer can do and how God answers every prayer."

> Ron Thomas, Pastor
> Rodgers Baptist Church, Garland, Texas

"Dr. Briney's two books HOPE and PRAY will inspire you to pray. If you feel discouraged about your prayer life, these books will give you hope to pray and wisdom to pray more effectively. You will not be disappointed."

> Doug Hammett, Author and Missionary
> South Africa

"Dr. Briney is a scientist by training. He uses the same disciplined, scientific methodology to prove God's promises about prayer. You will discover truth and insights gained from his personal journey with God, cancer, and prayer."

> Lester Hutson, Retired Pastor and Author
> Houston, Texas

HOPE

LESSONS FROM A CANCER SURVIVOR'S JOURNEY WITH GOD

DR. PATRICK BRINEY

HOPE: Lessons from a Cancer Survivor's Journey with God
© 2020 Patrick Briney

All rights reserved. Printed in the United States of America. No part of this publication may be reproduced, distributed, or transmitted in any form or by any means, including photocopying, recording, or other electronic or mechanical methods, without the prior written permission of the publisher, except in the case of brief quotations embodied in critical reviews and certain other noncommercial uses permitted by copyright law.

For information, please write:

> Permissions Coordinator, Life Changing Scriptures
> 2006 Mission Boulevard, Fayetteville, Arkansas 72703
> www.lifechangingscriptures.org/permission

Books may be purchased from Life Changing Scriptures for educational, business, or sales promotional uses. For information on quantity purchases, please write:

> Educational Purchases, Life Changing Scriptures
> 2006 Mission Boulevard, Fayetteville, Arkansas 72703
> www.lifechangingscriptures.org/bulk-purchases

Book 1 in this series: HOPE: Lessons from a Cancer Survivor's Journey with God / Patrick Briney

Book 2 in this series: PRAY: How God Answers Every Prayer / Patrick Briney

1. Religion 2. Christian 3. Prayer. I. Title.

ISBN: 978-1-951169-00-8

Scripture quotations are from the King James Version of the Bible.

Cover design and interior layout by Exodus Design Studio.

CONTENTS

Preface	I
Bad News	1
How Did I Get Here?	31
Prayers that Move Mountains	65
My Mountain	113
A Bigger Mountain	145
Pray Well	165
Epilogue	175
Appendix	181
Glossary	189
The Author	193

PREFACE

This story began more than thirty years ago when I asked God to teach me about prayers that move mountains. He taught me through faith, His Word, and the experience of cancer. He gave me a mountain to put into practice what He had taught me. Thank you, Lord, for your faithful and loving answers to prayers just when I needed them.

To my wife and family, Mom and Dad, brother and sister and their families, my church, and friends near and afar, thank you. I am grateful for your loving support during those tough times.

The story behind this book is interesting. In August of 2018, Colleen and I had dinner with our good friend Patty Minor, who had been encouraging me to write a book about my experiences and my studies in practical Christianity. The Lord gave me the green light, and a team formed from members in our church. Patty served as our project manager, Mary Saldivar as our editor, Adriel

Wiggins as our distribution consultant, and Pablo and Lisa Pagliani as our design consultants. Great friends in my weekly Bible study sessions prayed for me and provided helpful discussions and feedback. I am grateful to each one. What did I do? The usual—a little of everything. But most importantly, I told the story of what God taught me about prayer.

Thank you for taking time to read this book. My hope and prayer is that you too will discover the power of prayers that move mountains.

I studied prayer in the Bible and prayed to know more. I was baffled by the promise Jesus made about praying and moving mountains. I wondered if ordinary people could pray and expect God to do the impossible for them.

I learned firsthand that with God all things are possible. Even death, though inevitable, can be delayed. More than thirty years have passed since my bout with stage 4 Hodgkin's lymphoma and subsequent reoccurrence. God taught me about prayer and about hope in Him. My desire is that this book will give you hope. And I pray that you will share the things you learn with others.

I am a cancer survivor. And as you will learn in this book, the entire experience of cancer was an answer to my request to understand prayers that move mountains.

Pat

PREFACE

TIMELINE OF PERSONAL EVENTS

- 1956 March, Birth day
- 1974 August, UC Irvine
- 1974 December, Joined Christian group
- 1975 August, Began praying to find a church home
- 1977 January, Transferred to UA
- 1978 May, Graduated Zoology, B.S.
- 1979 September, Married Colleen
- 1981 March, Ordained to the Gospel Ministry
- 1983 May, Graduated Microbiology, M.S.
- 1986 May, Graduated Microbiology, Ph.D.
- 1988 March, Began praying to understand prayers that move mountains
- 1988 May, Symptoms appear
- 1988 September, First daughter, Lisa, was born
- 1989 March, Completed study on prayer and diagnosed with Hodgkin's lymphoma
- 1989 October, Completed chemotherapy
- 1992 August, Second daughter, Tenille, was born
- 1994 October, Reoccurrence of Hodgkin's lymphoma
- 1995 April, Last chemotherapy treatment
- 2020 March, published books to tell my story

1
BAD NEWS

Is any among you afflicted? let him pray.
— James 5:13a

I gripped the arms of the cushioned chair in the doctor's office to keep my fingers from running over the tennis ball-sized lump in the back of my neck. I'd been waiting days to hear the results of the battery of tests the doctor had been conducting. There had to be another explanation besides cancer for what could cause such a large mass. Was it an infection filled with pus or fluid? Could it be a hematoma from an injury I hadn't realized I'd sustained? It had to be something, anything but cancer.

The doctor entered his office, nodded by way of greeting, apologized for being late and sat in a chair facing mine. "Pat," he said. I could tell right then from the tone in his voice that the news was not good. "It appears as though you could have Hodgkin's lymphoma."

Just the mention of cancer sent my mind into a blur of thoughts about pain, sickness, tears, sorrow, surgery, and death. Nonetheless, I clung to his words. *If it appears as though I may have cancer, then there's a chance that I may not have it.*

"Tell me everything about it," I asked of him.

He talked while I listened for about ten minutes. By the time he was done explaining about what most likely caused the mass on my neck, I felt a strange kind of comfort. If it were the kind of cancer my doctor thought it might be, it was beatable. I asked more questions about Hodgkin's lymphoma and the strategy of tests to come to determine exactly what was wrong with me. Oddly enough, my main concern was the prospect of surgery. I did not want to go to the hospital, and I did not want to be put under and cut on. If only I could take a pill to resolve whatever was wrong with me.

"Do you think surgery is in the picture?" I asked.

Unanswered questions raced through my mind. But that's the way I am—intensely curious and needing to know and understand everything I am involved in. Before I was out of the doctor's office, I was already planning what to do in the library. Because I lived only two blocks from Mullins Library at the University of Arkansas, the library was practically my home away from home. It was my resource for knowledge and information. I could easily get lost in books of all kinds on any topic. But not today. I had to find out more about Hodgkin's lymphoma.

If only I knew for sure....

I started the car and headed home where my wife, Colleen, was waiting to hear what the doctor had to say.

1988 FLASHBACK TO SYMPTOMS

I was told that I had cancer in 1989. I had been sick for a year before I was finally diagnosed correctly. For a year I fought fatigue and sickness. The doctors told me I had a cold or a sinus infection. Little did I know, cancer had been spreading throughout my body. I had been studying what the Bible taught about prayer. I had asked God specifically to teach me about the prayers that move mountains. One week after I finished my study on prayer, I was finally diagnosed correctly.

About four weeks into my study on prayer, I developed what I thought was a bad sinus infection. I was suffering from headaches, sinus pressure, and a persistent cough. Little did I know at the time, God was answering my request that He teach me about prayers that move mountains. That was in March of 1988.

> *About four weeks into my study on prayer, I developed what I thought was a bad sinus infection.*

After several experiences of having doctors tell me whatever I had would run its course, I started to avoid going to the doctor when I didn't feel well and focused on the ministry instead. That spring, I drove to Chicago to visit a church to share my vision and work as a collegiate missionary. On the way, I developed an unproductive, nuisance cough, which I attributed to sinus drainage. After spending the weekend in Chicago, I traveled to the southeast corner of Indiana and stayed a week with the pastor of a country church, a good friend of mine. He mentioned, sometime later, that one morning he thought I looked very pale. I also had noticed that, some mornings when I looked in the mirror, I was pale and drawn. But that is not unusual if I am tired due to long, active days and only a few hours of sleep each night. When I returned home a week later, I was tired and glad to rest.

Throughout the summer, my cough and sinus drainage persisted. It did not seem to be getting worse, and at times I thought I was just about to recover. I'd had a sinus infection a few years earlier and had gone to see a doctor about it then. He had given me an antibiotic, and I had recovered. I did not feel as bad as I did then, so I saw no point in visiting a doctor about such a minor problem.

Being a missionary, I had a full schedule every day. I studied, prayed, prepared lessons, counseled, visited people, taught Bible studies, organized activities, wrote articles, cleaned the church, maintained our campus center, tried to be a husband, prepared seminars and deputation schedules, and so forth. In the fall, I spent more time visiting college students in the evenings and teaching studies. During the day, I was a volunteer biology teacher at the Fayetteville Christian School. The pace was hectic, but I loved what I did and still do. Being a part of helping others to know Christ and to grow spiritually is the most important and rewarding thing I have ever done. Unfortunately, my stamina and strength were declining. Maintaining a vigorous schedule was increasingly more difficult.

By July of 1988, I was experiencing night chills and sweats. I refer to this experience as the "Hodgkin's shakes." Within an hour of going to bed, I became very chilled, which caused me to shiver and shake. Breathing the air chilled me to the bone, so I made a tunnel with the blankets to the outside air and huddled next to Colleen. Colleen did not appreciate my shaking the bed. She laid extra blankets under me and over me and turned up the heat on the water bed. These nightly shivers wore me out and robbed me of sleep. The intense shaking was exhausting. Then, sometime during the night I would fall asleep, and early in the morning I would wake up drenched in sweat.

"This sinus infection is wearing me out, Colleen."

"You should go see the doctor."

"I guess so, but I am sure that once I go, he'll tell me that the infection has run its course."

Sure enough, after a couple of days of the shakes, I was feeling better. But the chills and sweats were recurring about every three weeks and eventually increased their frequency to every other week. Each episode lasted a couple of days longer. My energy level was seriously declining. I taught biology in the late mornings and came home exhausted. Instead of eating lunch, I was sleeping in bed so I could keep up with the late afternoon and evening activities.

Unfortunately for the kids at school, my wife, and others whom I worked closely with, my patience level was decreasing too. I was getting moody. So I finally went to see a doctor in September. I told him about my sinus infection that began in May and about the night chills and sweats. As I expected, he prescribed an antibiotic, and I went home.

In September, our first daughter, Lisa, was born, and it was a happy time. Family came to visit, and Colleen's mother spent a couple of weeks each time she came and was a big help to us.

The deception of Hodgkin's lymphoma is that the symptoms come and go in cycles.

The antibiotics appeared to work because my chills and sweats stopped. But this lasted for only about three weeks. The deception of Hodgkin's lymphoma is that the symptoms come and go in cycles. By the time the doctor saw me, I was at the end of the cycle of symptoms. I naturally attributed the improvement to the antibiotics. After all, I had a lingering sinus infection, I kept telling myself.

In November, I saw another doctor. I was sick and exhausted. I could not shake off this "infection," and the nightly chills and sweats were draining me of most of my energy. Colleen was beginning to get grumpy because I was keeping her awake and she was trying to take care of a new baby. I shook the bed for hours shivering and then soaked the blankets with sweat. I began sleeping in another bed for Colleen's sake. However, this meant sleeping on a regular mattress, and the night sweats were so bad the mattress was getting soaked. We had to set it outside during the day to dry it out.

I told the doctor my history since May, and after listening to my breathing, he diagnosed me with atypical pneumonia, which is caused by a bacteria rather than a virus. I should have asked him how he could come to such a conclusion without a culture, but it was the end of the day. I was tired, he was tired, and I was the last patient. Normally, I ask doctors and nurses more questions than they care to hear. But I wasn't talking much that day.

I took my antibiotic, and the next two nights I doubled the sweat output. I thought that the doctor probably diagnosed me correctly. I had pneumonia, and I was experiencing the pneumonic crisis characterized by sweating. Three days later, I felt better. Two weeks later, Colleen, the baby, and I were on our way to California to spend Christmas with our families. I was feeling much better.

However, the week after Christmas, I was relapsing into chills and sweats. My cough was getting worse. I visited a doctor at a hospital in California.

"This sinus infection is the worst I have ever had. I can't seem to shake it. I already developed atypical pneumonia because of sinus drainage into my lungs."

"Let me do a chest x-ray and a TB test on you. I am concerned that this has persisted so long," the doctor told me.

"Are there any other causes for my symptoms?"

"Well, if your cough and chills and sweats do not cease when you get back to Arkansas, I recommend that you go see a lung specialist."

He prescribed antibiotics, and the chills and sweats ceased until February. In the meantime, I finished my study on prayer and began writing transcripts for my radio program called Life Changing Scriptures.

1989 PAIN IN THE NECK

I'll never forget the big snow in February of 1989. The schools were closed, and most of the businesses were closed. That morning I was sitting at the table with Colleen, rubbing my right shoulder. It was sore, like a pulled muscle. I massaged it, trying to think what I had done. In the previous few months, I had been getting sore from playing volleyball on Friday nights. But this was Wednesday, and my shoulder was getting sorer instead of better.

As I rubbed my shoulder, I felt the edge of a large lump.

"Wow. What's that on my neck?" I felt a large, round bump at the base of my neck. I poked on it more and then went to look at it in the bathroom mirror. As I pulled back my shirt collar, I was shocked.

Most doctors' offices were closed due to the snow, so Colleen used the yellow pages to locate a doctor, and a few hours later I was in his office.

As I sat in the examining room, Dr. Steve Wilson walked in reading the nurse's description of my symptoms as I had told her. After examining me, he said he wanted to run some tests. He prescribed an antibiotic and told me to come back if the lump did not go away in a couple of weeks. Does that sound familiar? The lump decreased in size slightly, and the pain decreased. But after a week, I decided to go see a head and neck specialist, Dr. Fincher.

He thought it was a cyst but wanted to speak with Dr. Wilson about it. After conversing with him, Dr. Fincher instructed me to go back to Dr. Wilson's office and have more blood work done before they would biopsy the lump.

I left Dr. Fincher's office and drove to Dr. Wilson's office. *Biopsy*, I thought. *This could be more serious than I realize.*

After giving blood for the tests, I talked to Dr. Wilson more about the possible diagnosis. It was during this meeting that Hodgkin's lymphoma was first mentioned.

After a couple of weeks of tests and waiting for results, Dr. Wilson called me.

"The blood tests show no signs of an infection."

"So what is the next step? Biopsy?"

"Yes. We have eliminated the other probability of infection."

"Can I have Dr. Fincher do the surgery? He must be good if he does plastic surgery as a head and neck specialist."

"I'll call him right now and set up an appointment for you."

The following week, I was on the surgery table. Since the pathologist was at the hospital, Dr. Fincher was able to confirm to Colleen immediately after surgery that I had Hodgkin's lymphoma. The next day, I talked to Dr. Wilson about what to do next. He arranged for me an immediate appointment with Dr. Hayward, the only oncologist in Fayetteville at the time.

LIFE IN SLOW MOTION

Typically when we hear bad news, we go into shock. Our bodies and minds have to process information. There is denial, but there are facts. There are people to tell, but how to tell them and when? There are questions that come to mind. What will it be like to die?

Will it be painful? Will it be quick or slow? What will my quality of life be like and for how long? It becomes difficult to retain information and to think. One short thought is all that can be handled.

In my case, as a new father of a seven-month-old baby, I had to think about what to do for Colleen and Lisa.

HOW DO YOU SAY I HAVE CANCER?

The day Dr. Fincher had recommended a biopsy, it had taken only fifteen minutes to drive home, but it was a long fifteen minutes. Questions and decisions flooded my mind. I was thinking about wrapping up life already and at the same time processing how to survive. It was the proverbial hope for the best and plan for the worst.

One of the most difficult things I have ever done was tell my family and friends that I had cancer. During the discovery phase, I had been optimistic about fighting an infection. But when no infection was found and a biopsy was suggested, I realized this could be serious. I kept Colleen informed. But until there was a definite diagnosis, there was no need to talk to anyone else.

When Dr. Fincher had first mentioned the possibility of Hodgkin's lymphoma, I was shocked. It was unexpected. I suddenly felt like I was in slow motion. I felt very disoriented and yet very thoughtful. I was thinking about the next steps to take, what I should learn about lymphoma, how much time it would take to confirm the diagnosis, and how I would tell Colleen the news.

As a new father I had to think about what to do for Colleen and Lisa.

During my drive home that day, I tried to clear my mind of the melodrama unfolding in my thoughts. I kept reminding myself that there was nothing to worry about. God was in control, and I had given my life to Him. I was truly in good hands. Besides, the diagnosis at that point was not confirmed with a biopsy yet.

I prayed, collected my thoughts, and walked into the house to tell Colleen the news.

"Cancer?" Colleen asked, standing motionless after I gave her the good news, bad news speech I had rehearsed.

"Well, the doctor said he didn't know what it was. It is probably an infection."

"Are you saying it is not cancer?" she asked, her voice full of emotion.

"Well, there are other possibilities." I was beginning to regret having mentioned the possibility of cancer. Her face showed shock, and her voice was intense and demanding. I did not want to talk about the possibility of cancer to myself, much less anyone else, especially since there was nothing confirmed to talk about yet.

"So, when do the tests begin?" Colleen continued.

"Tomorrow the nurses will send my blood to the lab for tests."

A week later, as I was recovering from the surgical biopsy in the post-op room, Dr. Fincher told Colleen that he had looked at the biopsy sample under the microscope during surgery and had seen the cancer cells. Several days later, the clinical report from the lab returned with the official confirmation of Hodgkin's lymphoma.

When I called my parents, Mom was out, so I told Dad. We chatted about the weather and a variety of things, and then I told him the news. I do not remember much about that conversation except that I quickly qualified the bad news with the good news that Hodgkin's lymphoma is a very treatable cancer. Later, my mother called, and I remember that she was definitely upset and subdued. I reassured her that this was a treatable cancer. My parents told the rest of my family for me, which I was glad of.

I met my pastor, Brian Disney, at the KOFC radio station in Fayetteville, Arkansas. We went into the recording room, and I told him that I needed to make a prayer request known to everyone in the church. I told him about the cancer, and he told me that he was confident that the Lord would see me through this. I told him of the events leading to a confirmed diagnosis. A prayer request on my behalf went through the church prayer line immediately. I dreaded going to church the following Sunday morning. I did not know how to act, and I did not know if I could bear the expressions of concern and grief of three hundred people.

I was still feeling melodramatic about the whole thing and had not sorted out my own feelings. The night before Sunday service, it snowed several inches, so there was less than half the congregation in attendance. Being in a small Southern town, people are not accustomed to driving in snow and ice, and the city is not equipped to clear the roads very quickly. I came to church late so that I would not have to face people first thing in the morning and sat in the last pew as the congregation was singing. The hymns of heaven and Christ were a comfort to me. I started to sing, but choked on the words. It was enough to stand there and meditate on the words.

As Pastor Disney walked by, I stopped him and asked him to tell everyone thank you for their prayers. He made the announcement that I had something to say to everyone and invited me to the pulpit. For most people, church is a social function, and few people really know each other. But at Mission Boulevard Baptist Church, we are like a big family. Also, I had been there for fifteen years, from the time the church was just a year old. The average age of our congregation in the beginning was twenty-five years old. I was the first among us to have cancer. This was no light thing, and it affected the entire church. It was difficult to keep my composure in the pulpit that morning as people who loved me were crying, and I saw sorrow in their faces.

News of my cancer spread throughout the world as missionaries and pastors I knew were told. Letters and phone calls of encouragement came daily. It was much easier for me to talk to people about my cancer after they knew about it.

If you are going through the discovery phase with the prospect of finding out that you have cancer, consider talking to someone close to you about the possibility of something being wrong. This will give you and others who will be affected by the news time to brace for the possibility of bad news.

The first time I went to see the doctor about my health concerns, cancer was not even in my mind. So in my case, there was not much time to process the news. When Dr. Fincher said biopsy, I realized for the first time, this could be bad. I told Colleen what was going on, but our discussion and thoughts were hopeful. Being tested for cancer does not mean you have cancer.

But what if you are told that you do have cancer? I have thought about what I did, and I read about what others have done. Though different people have their preferences, there are at least six things most people agree on.

1. Call the people closest to you, such as family members.
2. Let those you tell pass the word on to others.
3. Talk to children and teens in a simple and matter of fact manner. Give them time to process the news.
4. Use websites and social media to inform and update friends with news.
5. Let people know that you are being treated, if this be the case. Many cancers have good success rates.

6. Give people time to adjust to the bad news. Different people will respond differently to the news. Many will not know what to say. Be appreciative, knowing that your friends, regardless of what they say, are trying to be helpful and supportive.

HOW TO TALK TO SOMEONE WITH CANCER

People are different, so there is not one way to talk to people with cancer. Being in the oncologist's office is interesting. I saw men and women of all ages in a variety of dispositions. Some were very weak physically, unable to walk on their own. Others looked like there was nothing wrong with them. Some were laughing, and others looked despondent. All were coping with the disease in different ways. Some were just discovering they had cancer; others were learning that they were in remission.

I walked past an open door and saw a family in the room around a patient. The doctor had just told them bad news, and the grief and crying was very, very painful. I wanted to walk in and be supportive. I felt compelled to be helpful, but it wasn't my place as a stranger to them to step into the room. When the doctor came to my room, I told him that I would be willing to help in some way. There was no hospice or support clinic in our area at the time. Where could people go to get support if they had no church family and pastor?

When I was told that I had cancer, I was not in despair to any degree like what I saw in that room. I was in emotional shock and tried to process what I was going to do. But that is my way of coping with bad news. I go into fix-it mode. Others need time to process their feelings. Some even give up.

During my first round of chemo, I was one of three patients being treated for Hodgkin's lymphoma. I always asked the doctor how the other two were doing. I was surprised when he told me one day that one of them had decided to stop the chemo. I cannot imagine giving up. But the side-effects were too much for the other guy to handle, so he stopped seeing the doctor. That was just unbelievable to me. The suffering a patient endures is temporary. Fortunately, the medicines used today give a lot of relief to chemo patients.

Obviously, everyone responds differently to personal crises. We all feel different, react differently, and think differently. Our bodies react differently to treatments. There are different cancers, different stages of cancer, different organs affected by cancer. The prognosis is different from patient to patient, and the support each patient has is different. And so I offer the following list of simple, general considerations to keep in mind when talking to someone in crisis.

1. Visit, send a card, give a cupcake, and do something to help, such as rake the lawn.
2. Call before you visit. Ask if there is something they would like you to bring.
3. Be kind and supportive.
4. Ask questions and listen. You don't have to know what to say.
5. Allow them to share their personal experiences and feelings.
6. Avoid telling them how they should feel.
7. Share poems, comics, articles, etc.
8. Give comfort. Grief is an emotional response, like your body going into physical shock. It takes time to recover from emotional trauma.
9. Be encouraging and reassuring that you are praying and desire to be helpful.

10. Find out what they need or would like.

11. End your conversations by saying you will be in touch soon.

INSIDIOUS DISEASE LIKE SIN

Hodgkin's lymphoma is a deceptive disease because of the symptom cycles of illness and wellness. I was treated for symptoms, but the root cause was not detected or treated until I was already in stage 4 of the cancer.

This is the way it is with sin. We seek to treat symptoms but neglect the root cause of our problem. We do not have to ask ourselves why we have problems. The answer is simple. We are sinners. We sin. We are born into the human race of sinners. As the psalmist David said in the Bible, we are born and "shapen in iniquity" (Psalm 51:5).

Okay, I know some object to the idea of babies being born in sin. But the Bible also says that babies are born innocent. How is it that babies can be born innocent, when the Bible says they are born and shapen in iniquity?

Here's how it works. The Apostle Paul says of himself in Romans 7:9, "For I was alive without the law once: but when the commandment came, sin revived, and I died." The Law Paul refers to is the moral Law of right and wrong that everyone is born with. Paul wrote in Romans 2:15 that the Law is written in the heart of everyone. This Law is represented in part in the Law given to Moses and Israel known as the Old Covenant, which is also referred to as the Old Testament.

Paul was alive before the Law? What does that mean? How could Paul have been alive before the Law? God gave Israel the Law and the Ten Commandments more than 1,400 years before Paul was born. And God's moral Law has existed since eternity past. So how is it possible that Paul could have been alive before the Law?

Paul was alive as long as he was not aware of the Law. He is referring to being spiritually alive, which is all about his relationship with God. During this time, he was innocent. He was not accountable to obey the Law. This is the period of time from birth to childhood prior to his being mature enough to be aware of and able to understand the Law. I will return to this thought about innocence and the age of accountability later.

FOUR PEOPLE GROUPS

IDENTITY	PHYSICAL		SPIRITUAL	
	ALIVE	DEAD	ALIVE	DEAD
BELIEVER	X		X	
BELIEVER DECEASED		X	X	
UNBELIEVER	X			X
UNBELIEVER DECEASED		X		X

First John 5:12 defines spiritual life and death, saying, "He that hath the Son hath life; and he that hath not the Son of God hath not life." In other words, those who have a relationship with Jesus Christ are alive spiritually. Those who do not have a relationship with Christ are spiritually dead.

Because it is possible to be physically alive or dead and to be spiritually alive or dead, there are four groups of people. The first group consists of those who are physically alive and spiritually alive. These, according to the definition in First John 5:12, are people who have a relationship with Jesus Christ. These are believers known as Christians.

The second group of people are physically dead and spiritually alive. These are Christians in heaven enjoying their relationship with God. Their carnal bodies do not go to heaven.

The third group of people are physically alive and spiritually dead. These are unbelievers, also known as the *lost*. They are alive physically, but because they do not have a relationship with Christ, they are dead spiritually.

And finally there is the group of people who are dead physically and spiritually. These are the condemned that choose an eternal existence separated from Christ. This is the worst-case scenario. There is no way to recover from spiritual death after physical death. Hebrews 9:27 says, "And as it is appointed unto men once to die, but after this the judgment."

PLAN FOR THE FUTURE

The time to plan for your future is right now while you are still alive physically. Now is the time to choose Christ and spiritual life before you die physically. Your eternal destiny is determined by the choice you make about Christ now in the short time you are alive physically. It is the most important decision you must make because of the eternal consequences.

Spiritual death is not the same as physical death. A physically dead body no longer functions. It cannot hear or communicate. It has no awareness. It is just an empty shell after the soul and spirit depart. But a dead soul separated from Christ is very aware. For example, Jesus tells of the rich man in hell using his spiritual eyes to see Abraham, having the ability to talk and hear, and he experienced pain. Spiritual death is not about ceasing to function. It is about being separated from your Creator, specifically from Christ. This occurs the moment you sin.

> *Spiritual death is not about ceasing to function. It is about being separated from Christ.*

The moment you are aware of the Law is the moment you know right from wrong. This is the moment you pass from innocence as a child to being accountable to God for choosing sin. This includes your thoughts of sin as well as your actions of sin.

Does this make you feel helpless and doomed? It should because this is God's purpose for writing the Law in our hearts. He wants to make us aware of our sins and our need to look for an escape from condemnation. He wants us to understand that we need His help.

First Timothy 1:9 says, "... that the law is not made for a righteous man, but for the lawless and disobedient, for the ungodly and for sinners." The righteous do not need the Law because they already fulfill the Law. The Law is for sinners to show them that they are sinners. Many sinners deny they are sinners. They need to be persuaded.

To show the Jews their desperate condition of sin, Jesus described impossible criteria for them to keep. In His sermon on the mount in Matthew 5:22, Jesus says, "But I say unto you, That whosoever is angry with his brother without a cause shall be in danger of the judgment: and whosoever shall say to his brother, Raca, shall be in danger of the council: but whosoever shall say, Thou fool, shall be in danger of hell fire." Saying to someone, Raca, is to call them stupid. To call them a fool is to say they are ignorant.

Have you ever despised or called someone a disparaging name? Have you ever been unkind? Have you ever called someone a fool? Then you have sinned. The ability to commit even one sin is evidence that you are a sinner. Everyone who commits sin is a sinner. Romans 3:10 says, "... There is none righteous, no, not one." And Romans 3:23 says, "For all have sinned, and come short of the glory of God."

> No one can be good enough to gain God's favor. Even the best fail to be good enough.

Most people try to be good, but they do not understand that they cannot be good enough. No one can be good enough to gain God's favor. Everyone falls short of being good enough. Even the best among us fall short. To make this point, Jesus told the crowd listening to Him in Matthew 5:20, "For I say unto you, That except your righteousness shall exceed [the righteousness] of the scribes and Pharisees, ye shall in no case enter into the kingdom of heaven." Can you imagine the stunned expressions on people's faces when they heard Jesus say this? His comment indicates that not even the religious leaders were good enough to go to heaven. If they were not good enough, then no one could be good enough!

Having knowledge of the Law is vital to helping people realize that they need help. The Law makes people aware of the consequences of doing wrong. A sinner who thinks he is not a sinner is not motivated to find a solution to his problem.

Did the Law exist prior to the time of Moses when God gave Israel the Ten Commandments? Yes. Did people who lived before Moses know the Law and know that they were sinners? Yes. Paul explains in Romans 5:13, "For until the law [the Law of Moses] sin was in the world: but sin is not imputed when there is no law." Sin is not imputed when there is no law. But people living before

Moses and the Ten Commandments all died. This means that the Law must have existed before Moses, and people living before Moses must have been aware of and accountable to the Law of God.

Similarly, Paul describes the time before and after he was aware of the Law, saying he was alive until the Law came. He was alive because he was not aware of the Law. The existence of Law does not condemn people. The awareness of not conforming to the Law condemns them. Thus, if there be no awareness of the Law, there is no sin. And because sin is the cause of death, where there is no sin, there is no death. Romans 6:23 says, "For the wages of sin is death."

Paul was innocent of sin until he became aware of right and wrong. This awareness occurs at the age of accountability.

Paul was spiritually alive as a baby into childhood because he was not aware of the Law, though he was born a sinner. This is what he means by saying he was alive before the Law. And then when he came to an age of maturity, he was aware of the Law, became accountable to it, sinned, and subsequently died. His nature of sin was the same. His thoughts and actions of sin were the same. But he was innocent of sin until he became aware of right and wrong. This age of maturity is often referred to as the age of accountability. It is at this time of maturity that Paul had a sense of guilt and shame.

The Bible does not specify an age at which people are accountable because people mature at different rates. For those who are developmentally delayed in their awareness and may never mature to that point while alive physically, I believe they will mature in their awareness after physical death and then be accountable for their sins. They will make their choice between Christ and sin, just as the angels did while they were in heaven.

THE PURPOSE OF KNOWING GOD'S LAW

Romans 2:14–15 explains that the Law is written in the hearts of humanity. It produces what is called a conscience. Paul uses as examples unbelievers (Gentiles), who are unaware of the Law of Moses. They set up their own laws and possess a conscience of right and wrong.

Paul says this is evidence that they are aware of God's Law. He writes, "For when the Gentiles, which have not the law, do by nature the things contained in the law, these, having not the law, are a law unto themselves: Which shew the work of the law written in their hearts, their conscience also bearing witness, and their thoughts the mean while accusing or else excusing one another." The making of laws and setting rules of right and wrong in a culture that has never known about Moses or Jesus is evidence that they know there is a standard of right and wrong. The thought of distinguishing between a right and a wrong is the result of moral awareness.

> *The thought of distinguishing between a right and a wrong is the result of moral awareness.*

By what means is it possible to accuse others of wrongdoing? Why do people feel the need to excuse behavior? The reason is that they have an innate sense of right and wrong. This is an awareness of God's Law written into the conscience of humanity. The sense of right and wrong is so strong that communities make up their own laws even if they have never heard of Moses. Then they break their rules. Why do people break their own laws? Because no one is righteous.

All people are born with a sin nature, but they are innocent until they become aware of the Law. Then, with that knowledge of right and wrong, they choose sin and immediately die spiritually due to God's separation from them. They remain spiritually dead until God saves them from their condemnation. God saves them when they believe Him that they are sinners, that they cannot be good enough to enter heaven, and that they are totally dependent on Him to show them mercy and grace.

The Law that humanity is accountable to is not the Law of Moses. As I mentioned earlier, it is the Law of God that has existed since before Moses and even before Adam was created. Romans 5:14 explains, "Nevertheless death reigned from Adam to Moses, even over them that had not sinned after the similitude of Adam's transgression, who is the figure of him that was to come." Paul is explaining that death occurred prior to Moses' receiving the Law of God. How could death have occurred from the time of Adam to Moses? It occurred because there was sin, which is the cause of death. And because there was sin, there must have been the presence of Law. Where there is death, there is sin. Where there is sin, there must be Law and the awareness of it. This is the Law of God that is written into the hearts of mankind (Romans 2:15).

The innate awareness of God's Law is manifested in knowing that there is right and wrong. This knowledge makes all of humanity accountable for their sins before God. Romans 1:18 says, "For the wrath of God is revealed from heaven against all ungodliness and unrighteousness of men, who hold the truth in unrighteousness." Where does the conscience of right and wrong come from? It comes from God. Why do all people have a sense of right and wrong? Because they carry within them the knowledge of right and wrong. This knowledge of right and wrong is the reason that everyone knows what it means to have a conscience and to feel guilt. Romans 1:19 says, "Because that which may be known of God is manifest in them; for God hath shewed it unto them."

God manifests Himself through faith and through physical creation. Through faith means that God reveals truths about Himself spiritually. Through creation means that God reveals

Study of the physical creation is a study of God. truths about Himself in the physical world. Romans 1:20 says, "For the invisible things of him from the creation of the world are clearly seen, being understood by the things that are made, even his eternal power and Godhead; so that they are without excuse." As more is discovered about the incredible complexities of the physical creation, its astonishing sophistication and intelligent design become ever more apparent. The study of the physical creation is a study of the mind and thoughts of God. Like an artist expressing himself in his paintings, God has expressed Himself and has revealed Himself since the beginning in His artwork called creation. As we learn more about the physical creation, we learn more about God.

ORIGINAL SIN

Some think humanity's sin is entirely Adam and Eve's fault. They think Adam is the cause of sin and death. It is just like sinners to blame someone else. But people do not die because Adam sinned. Romans 5:12 says, "Wherefore, as by one man sin entered into the world, and death by sin; and so death passed upon all men, for that all have sinned." Sin entered into the world of humanity because Adam and Eve were the first to sin. But death comes to everyone *only because everyone chooses to sin*, as did Adam. As Paul stated, "... all have sinned." There is no one to blame but us for sin and the death that follows.

Like Adam and Eve, we die spiritually; then we die physically. Spiritual death comes first. Physical death occurs later. It is this delay of physical death that makes it possible to be saved, to believe Christ, to repent, to confess that you are responsible for choosing to sin, and to ask God to forgive you. You will do this if you believe it.

Genesis 3 describes the circumstances of the original sin in humanity. And when I say original sin, I am referring to Adam and Eve's first sin. Satan was the first of all creatures to sin. Adam and Eve were the first humans to sin.

Death comes to everyone only because everyone chooses to sin, as did Adam.

Satan, in the form of a serpent, talked with Eve one day and asked her if God had told her not to eat the fruit of all the trees in the garden. She told him that they could eat the fruit from any tree, except for the tree in the middle of the garden. Eating that tree's fruit would result in death.

Satan told her that was not true and eating the fruit from that tree would actually open her eyes to know what God knows about good and evil (Genesis 3:5). Remember, awareness of the Law makes one accountable for obedience to it. Failing to keep *every command* of the Law, once you are aware, is sin. And sin brings death.

Eve considered how good the fruit looked and how it would make her wise to know good and evil, and she decided to disobey God. She ate the fruit and then shared it with Adam. Nothing is said about Eve's dialogue with Adam. Regardless of what was said, Adam chose to disobey God too.

Did they die? Yes. They had one point of the Law to obey. They knew that one point, and they disobeyed it. Once they ate the forbidden fruit, their eyes were opened, and now they were accountable to obey the whole Law. This accountability is what Paul was referring to when he said in Romans 7:9, "For I was alive without the law once: but when the commandment came, sin revived, and I died." Adam and Eve died spiritually. Physical death would come later.

With their eyes opened to know good and evil, Adam and Eve were accountable to all that they knew to be right and wrong. They were made aware of the Law of God written in their hearts the moment they ate the forbidden fruit (Romans 2:15). This is the Law that mankind becomes aware of at the age of accountability. This is the Law that makes all of humanity accountable to God. Satan was right about their eyes being opened to knowing right and wrong. He lied when he told Eve she would not die.

Do you know why it takes only one sin to cause death and condemnation? Romans 6:23 says, "For the wages of sin is death." It doesn't matter what sin you commit, just one will condemn you. James 2:10 says, "For whosoever shall keep the whole law, and yet offend in one [point], he is guilty of all." Adam and Eve are a perfect example of this. They knew only one point of the Law. They disobeyed it, became aware of all the Law, and immediately experienced spiritual death.

First Timothy 2:9 gives insight into why it takes only one sin to be guilty of all sins and to be condemned. It says, "Knowing this, that the law is not made for a righteous man, but for the lawless and disobedient, for the ungodly and for sinners, for unholy and profane, for murderers of fathers and murderers of mothers, for manslayers...." The law was not made for the righteous because the righteous keep the law. The righteous do not need to be told what to do. The righteous do right just like the unrighteous do wrong. It is not something they need to be taught. Why? Because they are righteous by nature. It is what they are. They *do* what they *are*. Because they are righteous, they possess a righteous nature, and they do what is right.

The Law was given to the unrighteous to show them that they are unrighteous. If you can commit one sin, then you do not have a righteous nature. Committing one sin is all the evidence you need to indicate that you are unrighteous. One sin of any kind, small or big, confirms that you have a sin nature. The problem is what you are, not what you do. What you do is simply evidence of the real problem, namely, what you are.

Adam introduced sin into humanity through birth. This is what David meant when he said, "I was shapen in iniquity" (Psalm 51:5). We are copies of the original couple. We carry the genetic code of Adam and Eve that gives us the same nature they had. We are seven billion Adams running around on Earth. Every person born into the world is a new Adam starting over again and again and again, first in innocence, followed by awareness of the Law, followed by death. *Adam* keeps repeating the same problem over and over again. Of course, being sinful, many deny they are sinners. This is the reason God gave humanity the Law. We are all sinners and must be convinced. Fortunately, there is a Savior to deliver us from the ultimate consequence of sin.

Adam was not created with a sin nature. He was created with a unique nature. It was unique, like all the angels were created unique. But unlike angels, Adam and Eve could reproduce themselves and make copies of themselves. More Adams could be produced, not by creation but by procreation.

What does it mean to have a sin nature? What is the difference between sinning and having a sin nature? It is the difference between doing sin and being sinful.

Adam was created with a nature that was capable of choosing sin. Until Adam and Eve chose to sin, their nature was not unrighteous. And at the time, they were aware of only one point of God's Law to obey, one sin to avoid. As long as they obeyed that one rule, they were not guilty of sin. Their nature was not sinful. But when they chose to disobey that one rule, their eyes were opened to know good and evil. At that point, they became sinners, and their nature was now *deemed* sinful. Their nature was deemed sinful when and because they sinned. Nothing about their nature changed. It was their choice to sin that changed their status from being righteous and innocent to being unrighteous and guilty.

Having a sin nature does not mean that you cannot choose to do what is right. Many people who do not believe in God choose to be kind, to tell the truth, and even send their children to church. They enjoy doing good. The problem with having a sin nature is that it will also choose to do what is wrong. It will sin; therefore, it is sinful.

Because all of humanity are replicas of Adam, all of humanity possess the same nature deemed sinful. Hence, the sin nature of humanity is the sin nature of Adam. We are Adam by birth. All of humanity are born and shapen in iniquity (Psalm 51:5). But no one is condemned until he or she becomes aware of the Law and chooses sin.

THE PROBLEM OF SIN

People often confuse being sinful with sinning. Being sinful is what you are. It means that you have a sin nature. This is the same as having an unrighteous nature. First John 5:17 says, "All unrighteousness is sin…." This means that if you are not righteous like God, then you are not righteous. He is the standard of what it means to be righteous.

Sinning is what you *do*. It is disobeying the Law of God. First John 3:4 says, "Whosoever committeth sin transgresseth also the law: for sin is the transgression of the law." If you disobey just once for any reason, you are a sinner. You commit sin because you are a sinner.

You can sin in both thoughts and behavior. In Matthew 5:28, Jesus said, "But I say unto you, That whosoever looketh on a woman to lust after her hath committed adultery with her already in his heart." Sinful thoughts are just as bad as sinful behavior in God's eyes because they both come from a sinful nature. This is what most people fail to understand about how to be good enough to go to heaven.

Sinning is the symptom, not the problem. Sinning is the result of having a sin nature. You might be able to change your behavior to obey God. You might be able to control your thoughts to not dwell on sin. But there is nothing you can do about having a sin nature. Being born with a sin nature means that you are a sinner. You are helpless to do anything about it. You are what you were born to be.

Jeremiah 13:23 makes this point, saying, "Can the Ethiopian change his skin, or the leopard his spots? then may ye also do good, that are accustomed to do evil." You cannot change what you are. If you were born unrighteous, then you are unrighteous, and there is nothing you can do about it.

Regardless of your behavior and your thoughts, if you have a sin nature, you are not good enough to go to heaven. Isaiah 64:6 declares, "But we are all as an unclean [thing], and all our righteousnesses [are] as filthy rags; and we all do fade as a leaf; and our iniquities, like the wind, have taken us away." All your righteousnesses are all the good things you do. They are nothing to God if you have an unrighteous nature. There is no such thing as your good deeds outweighing your bad deeds. Romans 3:20 says, "Therefore by the deeds of the law there shall no flesh be justified in his sight: for by the law is the knowledge of sin." God requires a righteous nature.

Because we cannot change our sin nature, it takes a miracle to be saved. God must save us. He alone can change what we *are* to what we need to be.

Unlike Hodgkin's lymphoma and many other cancers, sin has a known cause. We sin because we have a sin nature. It is this sin nature that explains why we sin. A sin nature *allows* us to choose to sin. It is the problem of what we are that explains what we do. Since the sin of Adam and Eve, humans have demonstrated that they are rebellious. We like to sin. Each of us, without exception, chooses sin. Granted, people choose to do good things too and know how to obey. But in spite of all the good that the best among us might do, choosing sin is still a problem. Romans 3:23 says, "For all have sinned, and come short of the glory of God." Without exception, everyone has a sin nature. Romans 3:10 says, "As it is written, There is none righteous, no, not one."

Is God to blame for sin? Some blasphemously claim that He is to blame. But this is not the case. God created man with the ability to choose to sin. After man chose to sin, then his nature was declared unrighteous. Man was not deemed unrighteous until he chose to sin.

Did God choose to make man sin? Did God make man unrighteous? No. God cannot sin, so He certainly is not going to make anyone else sin. Rather, He gave man a nature with the ability to choose sin. He did not give man a nature that could choose to do only that which is right or to do only that which is wrong. But He will give a righteous nature that only does what is right to anyone who will believe Him and choose salvation.

Some ask why God did not make man with a nature that couldn't sin. The answer is that God already made such creatures. They are the plants, rocks, and animals. They do what they are programmed to do without knowledge of any law saying they are wrong. Man is set apart from these because he has the ability to choose not to obey God. Rather than make more of the same that will only do what they are programmed to do, God decided to introduce into creation something with the ability to choose. He called this creature man. And before that, he created angels with the same ability to choose.

Some wonder why God made man, knowing that most would reject Him. But the answer is simple. God will not deny existence to those who will choose to enjoy eternal life with Him just because others do not want the same. It would be unjust of God to deny pleasure to some because others reject Him. Rather, God allows us to make our own choice and then enjoy or suffer the consequences of our choice. God does not allow the choice of some to deny others their opportunity to enjoy eternal bliss.

ACCEPTING THE NEWS ABOUT SIN

Just as it is difficult to hear that you have cancer, it is difficult to hear that you are a sinner. But denying either will not make them disappear. Sometimes, it takes a crisis to convince you to face the facts of your eternal destiny. Until you accept the news, you will not feel compelled to do anything about it. Solutions require accepting that there is a problem needing to be fixed.

Denying that you are a sinner does not make you less sinful. Saying that you are good enough to go to heaven does not make it so. Sin is a serious problem, and the treatment requires accepting the news that you need to do something about your sin problem.

People don't like to be told they are sinners. There are many who are outright evil and others who love to sin. They know they are sinners. Others try their best to be good. Many sincerely want to be good people.

No one is perfect. Unbelievers like to make this point clear to Christians. Many unbelievers are in denial or try to appease their consciences with the excuse that others are sinners too. But Christians have already admitted their imperfections. Being saved requires that one admit he or she is a sinner. This is what all Christians have done.

If God requires perfection, then anything less disqualifies us from entering heaven. And since everyone sins, it will take a miracle to get us into heaven. In fact, it will take mercy and grace.

2
HOW DID I GET HERE?

Come now, and let us reason together, saith the LORD.
— Isaiah 1:18a

I do not just want to believe in God, I want to experience God. I want God to be real in my life. I want His promises to be real experiences. I want to see God, to hear Him, and to touch Him.

I believe the Bible is God's inspired Word. I believe that its claims are true. When there is a claim made that I do not understand or do not experience, then I know that I am not thinking correctly about it. In order to think correctly about it, I must ask God.

I have had tremendous blessings from God with answers to prayers. I have had answers to questions about why God created us and have had Him place me where He wanted me to be. So when I wanted to understand the prayers that move mountains that Jesus spoke of in Mark 11:22–23, I was confident that God would grant my prayer. I was not surprised that He answered. But the answer and the method of the answer surprised me.

1964–1974   MY DESPERATE SEARCH FOR GOD

I was not always a Christian. I did not always pray. I wasn't even sure there was a God to pray to, but sometimes I prayed just in case. I figured it was better to be safe than sorry.

I remember first thinking about God in second grade. My parents sent my brother, my sister, and me to a small Christian school. It was here that I heard stories about Jesus and other Bible characters. I learned the books of the Bible, and I learned about the importance of asking Jesus to save us from sin and condemnation.

Mom felt that religious training was important. Her mother had died when she was five years old, and her father sent her to a parochial school. Religious values were important to her. She wanted moral training for her children.

I prayed a lot as a child, especially on stormy nights. I prayed hard. I prayed to be saved. I was frightened by the thunder. I cried myself to sleep during those scary nights. I would pray, "Dear Jesus, please save me. Please take me to heaven. Please don't let me go to hell."

I wasn't even sure there was a God to pray to, but sometimes I prayed just in case.

Fourth grade was not a good year academically, but I thanked Mr. Gordon for teaching me about Jesus. At the end of the last class of the year, I was outside walking away from the building with a compelling thought that I must go back and thank Mr. Gordon for teaching me about the Bible. I am sure I made his day.

Mr. Gordon had been a missionary in Africa. During some of our classes, he would tell stories about his experiences as a missionary. The most memorable class was the time he brought in chocolate-covered ants and fried grasshoppers. I ate a few grasshoppers and was amazed that they tasted like popcorn. But the chocolate ants never came near my mouth.

When I was in sixth grade, our family moved from Westminster, California, to Carbon Canyon in Chino, California. My mom sent my siblings and me to Sunday school at a little community church. I remember enjoying the flannelgraph Bible stories told by Mrs. Johanssen. She and her husband were a sweet elderly couple.

My dad sent me to church with questions to ask like "Who made God?" and "How do we know the words in the Bible mean the same thing today as when they were first written?" Mr. Johanssen was very kind and patient. I do not remember his answers, but he was sincere.

My dad is a skeptic, and that influenced how I looked at the world. He is an intelligent engineer who worked in the aerospace industry. He is inventive and always learning. He is a hardworking, practical, real-world guy. His skepticism is interesting because his father and mother were religious. His dad even studied for the ministry for a while before deciding to pursue a career as a medical doctor. Little did I know as a child that my life would take an ironic turn from that of my grandfather.

In junior high, I stopped going to church, as I began doing other things like participating in Boy Scouts. God was still in my thoughts, but I had doubts about His existence. I prayed and asked Him for assurance that He was real. But other than for Christmas and Easter, God was not a part of my life anymore. He was a seasonal character that people talked about and referred to.

In high school, I never shied away from talking to people about

God. I was interested in knowing why people believed in Him. The answer I received most often was that they just believed. I wasn't interested in "just" believing in something. I did not want to believe in something that was not there. But I did not want to reject God if He were there.

When I talked to friends about God, they would tell me that I should just believe. But why? Should I just believe because they believed? I could not understand how people could just believe for the sake of believing in something. To just believe did not work for me. I had already done that with Santa Claus and the Easter Bunny, and it turned out they were not real. Why would I want to live my life for something that did not really exist? For some, just believing was fine. But it did not work for me. I needed a reason to believe in God, and I wanted the assurance of His reality.

All through high school, I asked why I should believe in God. I prayed to Him often. I asked Him to show Himself to me. I did not want to *blindly* believe. I needed something real to believe in. I needed a reason to believe. I did not care if God did exist or if He didn't. I just wanted to know which way it was.

> If there were a God, I just wanted to know who He was and what He expected of me.

I felt driven to discover if there were a God. If He did exist, I did not want to be guilty of unbelief. I did not want to miss out on His will for my life. But I did not want to believe in a fairy tale either and ruin my life pursuing something that did not exist. If there were a God, I just wanted to know who He was and what He expected of me. But it seemed to me that to experience God required blindly believing in Him first. That was a hurdle I was not willing to jump over.

I did more than just ask friends about God. I searched for Him in science books as well as religious books. I read about Eastern religions and a variety of Western religious denominations. I read books about New Age spirituality and secular skepticism. I could not find a reason to believe or not to believe.

One evening, I sat in front of a burning candle at the kitchen table to apply a lesson in self-hypnosis to help me find God. I stared into the candle, repeating to myself, *there is a God … there is a God … there is a God*. After doing this for a while, I was still in doubt. That nagging doubt and uncertainty did not go away. So I reversed my approach, repeating to myself, *there is no God … there is no God … there is no God*. But that did nothing for me. Hypnotism did not resolve my doubt. I could not talk myself into believing in God, and I could not talk myself into not believing in God. I just did not know.

By the time I graduated from high school, I was frustrated about not finding a reason to believe or not to believe in God. I wanted to quit my search, but I wanted to have an answer. I just wanted a reason to believe.

I determined before I started college that I would make a decision one way or another. Then a week before classes began, I had an answer. I realized that I could not find answers because I had been searching for something that did not exist. That is why there were no reasons to believe. There are no answers for things that do not exist. Finally, I was at peace. I had a reason to believe that God did not exist. I was happy to have that settled.

> *I realized that I could not find answers because I had been searching for something that did not exist.*

1974–1976   MY PATH TO FINDING GOD

I chose to study at the University of California, Irvine with the dream of eventually attending their medical school. I loved the idea in general of helping people with medicine.

I developed this notion when I was eight years old. I was in the doctor's office being stitched up for a dog bite on my arm. I was lying on the table as the doctor was preparing to stitch me up, holding my breath, and closing my eyes. He was taking a long time to get started, and I asked him when he was going to begin, and he said, "I'm done." What? I didn't feel a thing. I looked at the eight stitches in my wrist in disbelief and said, "Wow, I want to do that." There was no pain. I thought it was fantastic to be able to help people not to hurt anymore. And so, from that day forward, everything I did was with the goal of becoming a doctor. And by the time I was out of high school, I knew I wanted to specialize in neuromedicine.

At UC Irvine, I majored in biology. I had always been fascinated by the mystery and power of the brain. UC Irvine had a good reputation for this field of study. As it turned out, the school was a training ground for atheists as well.

The first years of classes in history, literature, and philosophy involved exploring the themes of civil disobedience, morality, and why there was no God. There were plenty of reasons given not to believe in God. No rebuttals were given, and the arguments for the existence of God were not explored. Rather, when God was talked about, it was a subject derived from folklore in history and literature. There were plenty of stories about different views on gods and religions, but the Biblical teaching of God was absent. Christianity was not treated well as a topic at UC Irvine.

I discovered that other colleges also treated Christianity unfavorably compared to other religions. The summer after my freshman year at UC Irvine, I decided to take a comparative religion course with my high school sweetheart, Colleen. She was studying engineering at UCLA at the time. For the summer, we enrolled at a community college. In the class, we learned about many religions. We attended a Buddhist temple.

Christianity was in the last chapter, and it was not treated with the same respect as the other religions. Whereas the lessons on other religions were informative and positive, the chapter about Christianity was political and negative.

I asked the teacher why the book treated Christianity differently from the others. He said he never noticed that before. I was amazed that a college professor could be so blinded by bias. But in retrospect, after thirteen years of college study, I can say from personal experience that bias is rampant on college campuses. And when it comes to religions, Christianity in particular is a favorite target of ridicule.

And of course, as a student of biology, I was taught evolution. The foundation for this theory is the *presumptive*, philosophical perspective of naturalism. The argument is made that the origin of all things *must* be explained in the framework of physical laws regardless of evidence to the contrary. This presumption forces natural explanations, whether they make sense or not.

For example, the first and second laws of thermodynamics describe the behavior of the natural world, saying that energy cannot create or organize itself by natural means. These laws are well established and indisputable at this time. Science exploration and engineering inventions depend on these laws being inviolable. And yet, the universe is organized energy.

According to naturalism, somehow energy created itself and then organized itself into galaxies, star systems, and planets, all by natural means. Then molecules organized themselves into even greater complexity with the ability to harness energy and replicate. Life accidentally created and organized itself into existence by some natural means. Naturalism claims that all of this is a credible, scientific explanation for our existence in spite of its contradiction to the first and second laws of thermodynamics. The philosophy and bias of naturalism forces the acceptance of this irrational conclusion.

I accepted the theory of natural, evolutionary origins because I was an atheist. Naturalism was the only framework for me to work in. The contradictions were never pointed out in my classes. I was not challenged in the classroom to think about the underlying, philosophical presumption of naturalism. Looking back, I see that the entire academic culture was blinded, and continues to be blinded, by the bias of unchallenged acceptance of the presumption of naturalism. Attempts to challenge naturalism are quickly censored. The bias of naturalism blinds intelligent people from seeing contradictions in natural explanations and justifies, in their minds, contempt for the supernatural.

Evolutionists try to fit God's creation into their small, square box of thought.

ANSWERS TO MY QUESTIONS

In high school, Colleen and I did not talk much about religion. I was interested in searching for God at the time, but she was not. So we rarely talked about God or religion.

Then the unexpected happened. December 4, 1974, during our first semester of college, Colleen called to tell me that she had become a Christian. I said, "What? What have you done? Why did you do that? What did you do? How did that happen?"

It turns out that she had joined a Bible study group to learn more about God. She never told me about this. And we never talked about God, so when she called with this life-changing decision, I was caught totally off guard.

Colleen gave me the phone number of a Christian man at UC Irvine. She said he would be glad to visit with me and try to answer my questions. His name was Chuck Schwartz. He is the first person ever to challenge me to rethink my atheism by giving me reasons to believe in God. I told him that I was amazed to hear that there were answers to my questions.

I was especially amazed when he opened the Bible to read answers to some of my questions. It was the first time I ever saw the Bible used for some relevant purpose. In fact, I told him that I had owned a Bible all my life but had never known what it was for. This was the first time I saw it used to address real-life questions. By the time our meeting ended, I believed that there was a God. I later wrote about the answers I needed to hear in my book *Answers for Skeptics.*

Once I believed there was a God, Chuck shared with me a booklet called *The Four Spiritual Laws.* The first law states that God loves you and has a wonderful plan for your life. The second law states that humanity is tainted by sin and subsequently separated from God. As a result, we cannot know God's plan for our lives. The third law states that Jesus Christ is God's only provision for our sin. Through Jesus Christ, we can have our sins forgiven and can be restored to a right relationship with God. And the fourth law states that we must place our faith in Jesus Christ as Savior in order to receive the gift of salvation and know God's wonderful plan for our lives.

The booklet ends with a written prayer which says, "God, I know that I have sinned against you and deserve punishment. But

Jesus Christ took the punishment that I deserve so that through faith in Him I could be forgiven. I place my trust in You for salvation. Thank You for Your wonderful grace and forgiveness—the gift of eternal life! Amen!"

I was asked to pray this prayer, and I did. Why? I prayed because I believed in God. In that one meeting, Chuck was able to give me reasons to believe there was a God.

I prayed the prayer in that booklet because I thought that if I believe in God, then I should pray the prayer. But there was a problem. I did not know if Jesus was God. I was just happy to have a reason to believe that there was a God. So I prayed. Unfortunately, reading a prayer does not save your soul. I learned this lesson the hard way.

After my meeting with Chuck, I joined a Bible study group with some great guys. They were interested in Christian apologetics, which provides answers to questions about the Bible and God. This was exactly what I needed. We talked about the Bible and religious questions every week. Through these men, I met others involved in Christian apologetics and learned how to answer more questions. I even started teaching a Bible study.

The group I associated with was recruiting potential staff for their organization, but I was resistant to that idea. I had plans for medical school. I enjoyed learning answers to my questions and participating in evangelism projects, but I did not want to sacrifice my life goals and dreams.

During my time with the Christian Research Institute, Bob and Gretchen Passantino and Cal Beisner opened doors of experience for me to defend the Christian faith. On one occasion, for a week in southern California, Dr. Schonfield was hosted by the Long Beach College history department to market his book claiming that the resurrection of Christ was a hoax. I was amazed how a college professor could be so faulty in his thinking and write a book that was so easily dismissed.

I joined Cal and others to attend Dr. Schonfield's lectures at several college campuses in the area. Cal prepared a set of questions for our group to ask when given the chance. During one event sponsored by USC's philosophy department, I asked Dr. Schonfield how he could justify inventing a theory about Christ's disciples stealing Jesus' body and then looking for evidence, rather than first looking at the evidence to derive a hypothesis. I suggested that this was backward thinking. I had to ask him the question twice because he avoided answering the question.

THE PRESUMPTION OF NATURALISM

As an atheist, I had accepted the claim that the physical world created and organized itself. But saying something is so does not make it so. And during my time in college, I came to understand that there is no evidence to support such a claim. My atheism had been based on not being able to find a reason to believe in God. But believing or accepting something because you cannot find answers to your questions is pretty flimsy. As I found out, the lack of answers meant that I had not talked to the right people.

Ironically, I had accepted the belief of atheism based on what I did not know. I was guilty of the very thing I was trying to avoid. I did not want to blindly believe in something. Yet I was blindly believing in the presumption of atheism. This is the problem I saw in the college culture. In general, the culture blindly accepts the presumption of atheism without questioning it. And subsequently, it feels justified in off-handedly dismissing questions and evidence suggesting it might be otherwise. Worse yet, such a culture persecutes opposing ideas.

> *Ironically, I had accepted the belief of atheism based on what I did not know.*

It was contrary evidence and unanswered questions about

evolution and naturalism that bothered me. Our professors were great at presenting their one side of the story. But they ignored the questions and dismissed evidence for the supernatural as unworthy of scientific consideration. I thought that was intellectually dishonest. Blind acceptance of presumptive naturalism does not rationally justify dismissing evidence and censoring discussions that might contradict it.

My personal search for God involved considering all possibilities, not off-handedly dismissing Him. I was willing to examine my core beliefs and presumptions by questions such as *Is there more than a physical world?* I was even open-minded enough to listen to others present their cases for the existence of the supernatural and a God. Why not? That is what open-minded people do.

I was invited one evening to listen to a visiting professor talk about evolution and creation. I went to the meeting curious, but I left challenged. This was the first time I heard a professor present *the other side* of the story. He raised unresolved issues and presented the retracted claims about evolution. I was aware of some of the issues, but not all.

I left the meeting thinking *What else have I not been told?* That is when I realized that the information presented in the classroom was carefully selected with bias. Students were not being trained to think. They were being brainwashed to accept naturalism.

After thinking about it, I realized that I had bought into an atheistic theory and way of thinking that was worse than believing in God. What made it worse? The naturalistic explanations for origins contradict the laws of science.

For example, as I mentioned earlier, the first and second laws of thermodynamics state that energy cannot create and organize itself by natural means. Yet all of physical creation is organized energy. These laws that govern the universe are irrefutable. There are no exceptions, and there is no evidence to suspect exceptions will ever be found. Proposing that the world popped into existence and organized itself with the sophisticated design it possesses is absurd because the laws of science are contradicted. To insist on an explanation that contradicts the laws of science makes the proposal irrational and unscientific.

> Concluding that there is a supernatural intelligent Designer is based on what we do know from science, not on what we do not know.

I realized I had a reason to believe in an intelligent Designer based on the laws of science. I had a very good reason not to believe in the naturalistic explanation. No scientific explanation can be considered credible if it contradicts known scientific laws. It would be irrational for me to blindly accept the big bang story just because it is a naturalistic explanation. The laws of science indicate that the existence and organization of all things cannot happen by natural means. Concluding that there is a supernatural, intelligent Designer is based on what we do know from science, not what we do not know.

Based on scientific evidence and understanding, the rational conclusion for the existence of our universe is that it was intentionally designed by an intelligent, empathetic Creator. The explanation for a natural creation coming from nothing is absurd because it contradicts known evidence of the laws that govern the universe.

Censorship will not make the facts and conclusion for intelligent design go away. As long as serious questions and thorny challenges against naturalism remain unanswered, the supernatural explanation will not go away. These challenges must be addressed and debated in the science classroom.

THE PROBLEM OF SPIRITUAL BLINDNESS

So why do people insist on believing there is no God in spite of the evidence? How is it that intelligent people can prefer and insist on the presumption of naturalism in spite of the evidence suggesting otherwise?

Romans 1:21 explains, "Because that, when they knew God, they glorified him not as God, neither were thankful; but became vain in their imaginations, and their foolish heart was darkened." The Bible is clear that the problem of atheism or agnosticism is not due to not knowing God. It is a problem of rejecting God when they did know Him. This is a serious problem because rejecting God means that a person disconnects himself from truth. And once disconnected from God, memory of God fades. God is replaced with a *vain imagination*, meaning an invented, false explanation.

Disconnecting from God means you disconnect from truth. And when you disconnect from truth, you disconnect from Christ. Jesus said of Himself in John 14:6, "I am the way, the truth, and the life: no man cometh unto the Father, but by me." When this happens, you invent your own explanations to substitute for the real reason why we exist, what our purpose in life is, what is right and wrong, and what happens after death. The result is a darkened heart. This means that your explanations make it difficult for you to recognize and accept truth from God. Jesus admonished in Luke 11:35, "Take heed therefore that the light which is in thee be not darkness." Jesus warns about believing something that is false. This can be referred to as *dark light* or *false truth*. The danger of believing something that is not true is that you will be hindered from accepting truth when it is presented to you. In Matthew 6:23, Jesus says, "... if therefore the light that is in thee be darkness, how great is that darkness!"

My favorite Bible example of how a false perspective blinds people from seeing truth is found in John 18:38 when Pilate looks at Jesus and asks, "What is truth?" As he was staring into the eyes of Jesus, he was staring in the eyes of truth. Pilate did not recognize Jesus as truth when he looked at Him because what he believed was truth did not include Jesus. According to Romans 1:21 mentioned above, at some point in Pilate's life, *when* he knew God, he did not accept and glorify God. Rather, he chose to believe in other gods and in other invented notions called truth. The Bible calls these vain imaginations. Subsequently, his heart and mind were blinded from recognizing truth. Jesus did not conform to Pilate's accepted version of truth and was rejected.

Isaiah 5:20 describes how those who reject God can be so confused that they do not recognize right from wrong. It says, "Woe unto them that call evil good, and good evil; that put darkness for light, and light for darkness; that put bitter for sweet, and sweet for bitter!"

Pilate's experience represents my experience. I rejected God in my youth, and I continued to deny Him. When I heard truth, I preferred a different truth and looked for other gods. Eventually, I chose not to believe in God and accepted the explanations about our universe of those who did not believe in God. I came to a point, as many do, of asking God to prove Himself, to show Himself, and to convince me. The truth is that He already did reveal Himself, and I rejected Him. That is what made it more difficult for me later to recognize and accept His truths when I began asking questions about Him.

The Bible warns about the danger of rejecting God. For example, First Timothy 4:1–2 says, "Now the Spirit speaketh expressly, that in the latter times some shall depart from the faith, giving heed to seducing spirits, and doctrines of devils; Speaking lies in hypocrisy; having their conscience seared with a hot iron." Those described in the latter days represent the experience of all humanity when they reject God. In addition to people inventing alternative truths, seducing spirits also promote falsehoods to turn people away from God and Jesus Christ.

It is sobering to think that you could be confident that you are right when in fact you are wrong. This insidious condition is far worse than cancer. Proverbs 16:25 explains, "There is a way that seemeth right unto a man, but the end thereof are the ways of death." It is important to be humble and open-minded to listen to God and to receive His instructions. What you believe about Him and the Bible is a matter of eternal life and death.

It is a miracle that anyone gets saved once they reject God. But miracles do happen. God sees to it, especially when it comes to saving souls.

DOUBTERS

It is astounding how foolish some people are when they treat God and death with disregard. Some disdain God and flippantly say that they look forward to partying with their friends in hell. But where you spend eternity is no joke. Where you end up is forever. Life on Earth is barely the start of existence. Heaven and hell are eternal. Nothing is more important than preparing for your eternal destiny.

Even when I did not believe in God, I searched for Him. I did not dismiss the issue as unimportant. If there were a God, I wanted to know who He was, and then I wanted to know what He expected of me. I prayed. I asked questions. I thought a lot about how to determine His existence. It is irrational and foolish to dismiss the issue of eternity as unimportant. How many people will end up in hell because they arbitrarily decided that it was unimportant and nothing but a joke?

Some complain about feeling judged and condemned as horrible people because they are told they are going to hell. This attitude creates a serious problem. It is denial that there is a problem. As long as there is denial, finding a solution to the problem is neglected.

The Bible says all have sinned. All are unrighteous. God does not single out a group of people as being worse than others. He died for all because all are sinners and need His help. Without His death to pay the penalty of sin, no one would go to heaven. He made the ultimate sacrifice because He loves all.

> *If you think you are a reasonable person, then it is time to be reasonable with God.*

No one has to go to hell. God has a plan for salvation. His invitation is for anyone who will accept it. Only those who accept His plan will benefit from His plan. This makes sense. It is reasonable for God to allow people to make their own choices, as painful as it might be.

If you think you are a reasonable person, then it is time to be reasonable with God. It is time to take your eternal destiny seriously.

A DESIRE TO EXPERIENCE THE REALNESS OF GOD

Though I enjoyed the spiritual activities as a student at UC Irvine, I was disappointed with the academic experience. For one thing, the professors were not supportive. When I tried to talk to Dr. Lynch, the professor of psychobiology, in his office, all he did was blow his pipe smoke in my face, and then he turned his back on me. I walked out and never talked to him again. When I tried to talk to the chemistry professor, he told me that he had already explained the topic in class and would not talk to me. I never tried to talk to another professor at UC Irvine again.

The drumbeats of naturalism, evolution, and atheism were heard often in every class. We were taught in philosophy the reasons why God could not exist. In biology, we were taught that the only rational and scientific explanations for existence were restricted to naturalism regardless of the evidence. If I had not been introduced to Christians on campus who had answers, I would never have known that the dogmatic arguments for atheism had already been thoroughly refuted.

If I had not been introduced to Christians who had answers, I would never have known that the dogmatic arguments for atheism had already been thoroughly refuted.

I was not happy at UC Irvine. I prayed every day for about a year for God to show me where He wanted me to go. I told Him I would do anything for Him and go wherever He guided me just to see an example of ministry like that in the book of Acts.

During the fall semester as a junior at UC Irvine, my roommate's friend from Arkansas came to visit. After talking to him about my frustrations at UC Irvine and my prayers for a more real experience with God, I felt strongly that I needed to go to Arkansas. But I didn't even know where it was on the map. This was one of the last places I would have ever thought to go. But after spending time in prayer about it, I knew that I should go to Arkansas. Three months later, I was on my way to the University of Arkansas in Fayetteville with plans to pursue medical school. It was a miracle that I ended up in Arkansas.

Can you be too committed to God? Can you be too involved in serving Him? I worried about going overboard. But if God created me, then He is the one to live for and to look to for purpose in life. I just want to fulfill God's plan for my life. That is what makes my experience with God real.

Because my experience with God is real, I am committed to Him. To be less than fully committed to serving Him is unjustifiable. It is a denial of Him. That is unthinkable.

No one can do too much for God. After all, think about what God has done for you. He not only created you, He gives you guidance and opportunities to be blessed now and into eternity. I think you can *lack* in your commitment to serve God, but you can never be too committed. The more committed you are to God, the more meaning you have in your life. God's plan for your life is the best plan for your life.

God's plan for your life is that you love Him, grow in knowledge of Him, and serve Him. There is no greater calling than to serve Christ. All Christians are called to fulfill this plan for their lives regardless of their career choices or where they live.

Every Christian is a full-time minister, as the Bible says in Second Corinthians 5:17 and 20, "Therefore if any man be in Christ, he is a new creature: old things are passed away; behold, all things are become new. Now then we are ambassadors for Christ...." He expects every Christian to represent Him and to share His message of love, salvation, and eternal life.

My plan was to finish my last year and a half of college in Arkansas and then apply to medical school. But the Lord had other plans.

The first day I walked around the UA campus, I met students from the campus ministry of Mission Boulevard Baptist Church. The next day, I met my roommate, and he was a member of that same church. Two weeks later, I visited Mission Boulevard Baptist Church. Not long afterwards, I was participating in their campus ministry. I even met with the pastor every week for a Bible study. He had developed a series of lessons that not only answer important questions but that help people understand how to discover answers to questions. It was a perfect fit for me because every day I was asking new questions about God and the Bible. And then I began teaching Bible studies.

1977–1987 FINDING GOD

As I studied the Bible, I learned about belief and trust. I learned about salvation. Then I heard a sermon that God used to reach me.

The pastor used the illustration of sitting in a chair to demonstrate what it means to *believe* unto salvation. First, he explained how most people believe. He sat on a chair in front of the congregation, saying that many people believe in God with uncertainty. He was sitting on the edge of the chair as if the chair were about to collapse. He said he believed that the chair would support him, but he was ready to catch himself if the chair failed. This is how many people believe in God. They trust a little bit but are a bit uncertain. They want to trust God but are not confident He will save them. This is tentative belief, which is really unbelief.

He explained that in order to be saved, it was necessary to explicitly believe God without doubt and trust in His promise to give salvation, eternal life, and a future in heaven. God cannot lie, and He cannot be prevented from fulfilling His promise. So then, there is no reason not to explicitly believe Him. Having said this, the pastor sat back in the chair and rested comfortably. He said, "This is how to rest in the promise of Christ. Trust Him. Believe in Him. Let Him save you. And don't worry about it anymore."

Wow, I thought. *I've never experienced that*. I prayed a lot, and I prayed often, asking God to save me just to make sure. But I always had a nagging doubt in my mind. I had no doubt that God was able to save me. The question that nagged me was would He? Did He?

Remember the prayer I read from the booklet during my

> *I had no doubt that God was able to save me. The question that nagged me was would He? Did He?*

meeting with Chuck at UC Irvine? I read the prayer, but reading and believing are two different things. My prayers were not satisfying, and I was not confident in my salvation. So that evening, after church services, I went back to my dorm room and prayed.

"Lord, please save me. Please let me know that I am saved. Please get rid of the doubt in my mind. Please give me assurance. I want to know that I am saved." I prayed for two hours that evening with great intensity.

I went through a checklist of things that were necessary for salvation. "I believe that Jesus is God. I believe that Jesus died for my sins. I believe that He will do as He promised. I believe that He loves me and wants to save me. I believe that I am a sinner. I repent of my sins. I want to be delivered from my sins and the condemnation because of my sins. I believe that without Christ's help I will be condemned in my sins. I am sincere in my beliefs. I truly want Christ to be my Lord and Savior. I believe that He is merciful and gracious. Lord, please save me."

Did I believe enough? Did I pray sincerely enough? Did I say the right things? Did I overlook something?

I was exhausted *trying* to get saved that night. And eventually I was lying on the bed, praying and praying to be rid of my doubt.

Lord, I hate to do this, but it's late, I have a test tomorrow, and I am tired. I have to quit trying.

Immediately, I experienced relief and an assurance that I was saved. The thought in my mind sounded so loud and clear: "That is what I was waiting for." *What?*

I quit trying. That is what God was waiting for. Salvation is by grace, not by works. It is by grace from God, not by our efforts. I was doing my best to say the right things and feel the right way in order to gain God's approval. But by trying to say the right things and feel the right way, I was getting in the way.

Grace in the Bible means favor from God that is undeserved. Grace is commonly described as unmerited favor. By trying to say and do and feel the right way, I was offering God a reason to save me. I was doing all I could to show Him that I was at least *trying* to be as worthy as possible.

But if God saved me because I demonstrated that I was sincere enough and able to believe enough, then He would be obligated to compensate me for my effort. Receiving an earned reward is not grace. An earned reward is given in return for something done. There was nothing I could do for God to deserve a reward. All I could do was to ask God for help because I was helpless.

Worse than being helpless, I did not deserve to be saved. I was a sinner and unable to do anything to correct all the wrongs I had done. I deserved to be separated from God. I was a sinner and, therefore, was guilty of offending God. This means that I had offended an infinite being with infinite feelings.

How does a finite creature correct an infinite wrong? How could I possibly pay for such a debt of wrong? It is not possible. The wages of sin is death—eternal death. This was my dilemma. This is your dilemma. This is everyone's dilemma. We are all guilty of offending an infinite God by choosing to sin. The only acceptable payment for an infinite offense is an infinite payment. This is the reason hell is eternal. And this is the reason we need grace.

All I could do was ask God to forgive me, believing that He would save me. He did. That is grace. What about you? Do you believe in the grace of God, or are you still trying to be worthy in some small way to gain God's favor and blessing?

Saving us by grace means that God gets all the credit. He does all the work, and He shows all the nobility of forgiving an infinite offense and infinite debt. He gives us the promise of eternal blessings, though we deserve eternal condemnation. We should all be thankful that God is a loving God, willing to forgive and to show grace.

> God graciously gives us the most precious gift of all, which is salvation.

God graciously gives us the most precious gift of all, which is salvation. It is the most precious gift because the price that made it possible was the sacrifice of His Son, Jesus Christ. There is no way to describe the experience of eternal death. But God and His Son willingly experienced it to pay for our sins.

It is not possible to deserve such a gift, but God offers it to us free of charge. All we need to do is believe that He made the offer possible, that we do not deserve it, and that there is nothing we can do to earn it. We cannot be sincere enough, and we cannot believe enough to be worthy of it. Only when we stop trying to be good enough and let God save us as we are, as sinners, will God save us by grace.

I remember the moment I was saved like it was yesterday. For several years prior to that moment, I had agonized, trying to be saved, asking God to save me, and struggling with doubt. Then I quit trying. He saved me at that moment. I was at peace and had no doubt that God saved me.

Being the skeptic that I am, I had to put my new experience to the test. I paced around the room trying to talk myself out of the confidence I had. I repeatedly said, "I am not saved. I am not saved." But it was to no avail. I was saved. I thought, *Of course I am saved. What do I not believe? I believe everything God says.*

I pondered why getting saved was so hard when it is so easy. I still think about it to this day. I am so glad I gave up and let God save me as I was.

This is my testimony. I know God personally. I talk to Him. He talks to me. My relationship with God does not depend on whether others believe it or not. It is as true as the oatmeal I ate for breakfast the other day. I can't prove to you that I ate oatmeal for breakfast, but it is true nonetheless. I don't have to prove my experience to anyone else to make it true. I was there, and I can tell you, it was real.

> *I don't have to prove my experience to anyone else to make it true. I was there, and I can tell you, it was real.*

At the same time, you do not have to believe me. You do not have to believe the Bible. You do not have to believe God. But what you believe will not change what is true. It is up to you to search for God yourself. And the way to find Him is to pray. Ask Him to help you know Him.

God personalizes His experience with each soul through faith. This means He confirms by revelation His promise to you. Then you will answer to Him personally. Accepting or rejecting Him is a personal matter between you and God. Someone might tell you about God, but God alone personalizes the message to you by revealing Himself. By faith He confirms these truths in your heart. And when it is confirmed, you will be challenged to make a decision.

Because God personalizes His message to you by faith, you alone are responsible for the choice you make. Your choice is acceptance or rejection of God's personalized message and confirmation to you.

LIVING A NEW LIFE IN CHRIST

Unlike at UC Irvine, the faculty at UA were very friendly and easy to talk to. When I visited the head of the English department, he got up from his desk as I walked into his office and shook my hand. I was astounded by his kindness and wrote home about it. It was a welcoming environment.

I met and made new friends every day. Soon I was teaching Bible studies on campus.

A lot of people were very eager to learn about the Bible and have their questions answered. I knew what that was like, so I was glad to teach them and provide answers. Among the lessons I developed and taught was a series of studies developed by Pastor Brian Disney of Mission Boulevard Baptist Church. It is the best series of studies to establish Christians in the faith that I have ever been through. These lessons lay a foundation of systematic Biblical concepts that help people understand the Bible. This framework helped me deepen my insights into Biblical doctrines I had been taught during the previous two years of my Christian apologetic training.

These Bible Concepts were life-changing for me. With a proper framework to organize and explain doctrinal relationships, I was able to study the Bible, understand it, and reason out answers. Within a year, I put these lessons into study guides to help others teach them as well. By then, I was teaching eleven Bible studies and participating in eleven Bible studies each week.

I spent time every day praying on my knees at my bedside. I prayed for God's will to be done. I prayed for souls to be saved, for wisdom to answer questions and to teach Bible studies, for the comforting of people who were hurting, for God to use me more. I prayed for God to take me beyond my own limitations, to help me share His message more effectively, to be bolder in meeting people, and to be more surrendered. I did not want to miss out on anything God had planned for me, so I yielded myself completely to Him and prayed that He would help me be even more yielded. I wanted God to use me to the fullest extent, so much so that I asked Him to help me get out of the way to allow Him to live through me. His will and His way were all I wanted. There was no holding back. I determined to be 100 percent committed to Him.

I studied the Bible every day, wanting to learn as much as I could as fast as I could. I did word studies by looking up words of interest in *Young's Analytical Concordance* and reading every verse that contained those words. I read every verse in the Bible with the words *body*, *soul*, and *spirit* to discover the design and function of each. I read every verse in the Bible with the words *law, creation, God, Jesus, Satan, love, salvation, righteousness, sin, angels, disciple, evangelism*, and many more. I studied verses, chapters, books, and covenants. Every night I listened to recordings of Alexander Scorby reading the Bible. I created a reading of the Bible for my pocket recorder so I could listen to each chapter being read repeatedly until I was satisfied to move on to the next chapter. I immersed myself in the Word of God, prayer to God, and ministry with God.

The Lord called me to preach in the fall of my senior year, and I abandoned my plans for medical school. It was a very big disappointment to my folks and others who knew only of my plans for medical school. Everything I'd done since second grade was about going to medical school. So this was no small decision. But for me, it was the only thing to do.

God had answered my prayers to take me where He wanted me and to use me as He wanted. I could not have been happier. In fact, I was ready to drop out of school and devote myself completely to ministry. But under advisement of my pastor and the pleadings from my parents, I completed my senior year of school with a zoology degree.

I continued teaching Bible studies, counseling, and leading ministries in the church. I was leading the evangelism efforts on campus and coming up with new ideas to reach students. I was participating in as many church ministries as I could with the goal of eventually having personal experience in every ministry of the church. And during the building program for a new church building, I was there every day as time permitted.

After I graduated, I needed a job, but finding a job with a zoology degree was not easy. After being turned down by more than fifty potential employers, I eventually got a job in the UA student union. After a semester of washing dishes, I decided to apply for graduate school. I was accepted into the microbiology department to pursue a master's in microbiology. It was a means of earning a stipend, and more importantly, of meeting more students for ministry.

In 1980, I was asked to lead the church's discipleship ministry as the discipleship director. We had a very active membership engaged in Biblical discipleship just like in the book of Acts. Most members were teaching at least one Bible study. Services were full of visitors from these studies. All members were participating in ministry teams, which served as small groups in the church. Baptisms were regular events.

Eventually, our church ministry team leaders asked me for more lessons and direction beyond the church's Bible Concepts. Prayerfully, I developed a comprehensive discipleship training program which resulted in a seven-step training series for everyone from the lost to preachers. The combination of our one-on-one training and the discipleship studies was key to our discipleship success. Friendships were forged through personalized training, and commitments to Christ were deepened with insights into His Word.

I approached the ministry on campus as a mission effort rather than as a college/career class at church. Financial support came from churches to help us, so I spent time on deputation to present our ministry to other churches. I also offered training and wrote a booklet on how to start campus ministries so that other churches could start their own mission efforts at nearby campuses.

I began the three-week Summer Training And Mission Program (STAMP) for students and immersed them into discipleship training of doctrine, character, and ministry skills. Our campus center housed students, and our ministry was filled with activities every day.

EXPERIENCING GOD

The more I study the Bible, the more amazed I am. The Bible is such a wonderful book. The wisdom is astounding. Following its instructions has proven its lessons to be right over and over again. There is peace and contentment in living by the words of God. The Bible is a practical book about how to think and how to act. It gives the best advice on building relationships, marriage, family, children, and parenting. Living by Biblical values and embracing the Bible's philosophy of life is superior to all alternatives. I tell people that a lot of training that folks pay thousands of dollars for in annual leadership seminars is available in churches for free every week.

The Bible is the most quoted source for inspiration and guidance by the founding fathers of the United States. Even those who did not believe in God recognized the Bible's value to society. With its guidance, the greatest nation in history was built on a foundation of Biblical values. And on this foundation, a government was formed that allowed people to correct its problems.

One favorite lesson I teach in our Leadership Training Institute of America is about British philosopher John Locke's statement that if everyone would just live by the second command, to love others as yourself, people could truly enjoy maximum freedom.

Biblical values proved to be very practical and obviously beneficial. The United States is proof that the freest, most prosperous and generous culture is a culture of Biblical values. The Bible served as the standard by which wrongs could be corrected. The disparaging of the Bible and Christian values that is rampant in our culture today and especially on college campuses is an irrational idiocy that makes no sense.

As I stated earlier, I am not interested in merely talking about God. I want more than to talk about prayer. I want to experience God and granted prayers. This is the desire of my heart. The experience is what separates fact from fiction in practical living. Experience confirms God's presence and the reality of productive, practical prayer. This is how I want to live my Christian faith. I am not interested in the talk. I want the experience. Living by the teachings of the Bible and observing the lives of others who also live by the Bible convince me that there is no better way to live.

Fortunately, experiencing God does not require perfection or heroics in the faith, just down-to-earth practical experience. God does not require perfection and perfect prayers before He answers them. The Bible describes the amazing prophet Elijah, who experienced miraculous events as a result of his prayers, as a "man of like passions," meaning he was just like anyone else. King David committed adultery and murder. Moses was afraid to lead others. Jonah ran away from God when called upon to preach to the citizens in Nineveh. Adam and Eve chose sin even in the best of conditions. These and many more all suffered from the human weakness of lust, selfishness, and greed. But they all wanted to live for God in spite of themselves. And all experienced God. All experienced God's answers to their prayers.

You do not have to be a hero in the faith to experience God. You need only to commit yourself to God to live for Him, to desire His will for your life, whatever that might be. Don't be afraid of Him. Trust Him. Ask Him to help you trust Him.

PRAYERS THAT REALLY MOVE MOUNTAINS

As I said, I believe that if God makes a promise in His Word, then it is waiting to be experienced. But there was a verse with a promise and experience that was eluding me.

Mark 11:23 says, "For verily I say unto you, That whosoever shall say unto this mountain, Be thou removed, and be thou cast into the sea; and shall not doubt in his heart, but shall believe that those things which he saith shall come to pass; he shall have whatsoever he saith." I prayed for people to be healed, and I prayed for other things that were not granted. Friends died in the hospital, and membership in our ministry dwindled in spite of prayers. Some prayers for safety and ministry needs were not granted. I believed when I prayed, and others also believed. But our prayers were not granted.

I don't know how I could have been more believing, so I asked the Lord, "Teach me the prayers that move mountains." What does it mean to believe and pray for miracles to happen? If believing is all that is required, then why am I not experiencing granted prayers? Is it possible to really believe without doubt that something will happen, and God will grant it? If so, what was lacking in my belief? What could I do to believe the right way?

I saw and heard about amazing things happening, like the pastor's son being run over by a tractor wheel yet not being injured at all. I saw a baby in our church with no muscle strength who, after a special prayer meeting for him, showed no signs of disease the next day. The doctors marveled over him. But these miraculous prayers were not common.

My prayers bothered me because too many were unanswered. It made praying very difficult because it seemed to make little difference. Like many have expressed to me, prayer was disappointing and frustrating. It made it challenging to be faithful to pray. Answered prayers seemed so arbitrary. Why were some prayers granted and others not?

I felt that sincere prayers should be granted all the time regardless of the magnitude of the requests, especially those for the health and well-being of faithful, committed people serving God. There certainly was no doubt or lack of believing that God could grant any and every prayer. God can do anything.

But after disappointments of unanswered prayers, the question became does God want to answer this prayer? Does God want to answer my prayers? Is there something wrong with me?

Of course, I am not perfect, so there is always that explanation for why God may not answer my prayers. But then why did He answer my prayers at other times? I was still the same person believing that God could answer my prayers. Why did He answer some prayers and not others even though I earnestly believed every prayer? There was too much inconsistency to explain. The answers seemed haphazard and unpredictable.

If God says that prayers can move mountains, then I want to see mountains moved. I want to see what mountains He is talking about and how far they will move. I do not doubt that He can move mountains. Any doubt I have is in me, not in God.

In Malachi 3:10, God challenged Israel, saying, "… prove me now herewith, saith the LORD of hosts, if I will not open you the windows of heaven, and pour you out a blessing, that there shall not be room enough to receive it." And in Isaiah 1:18, the Lord says, "Come now, and let us reason together, saith the LORD: though your sins be as scarlet, they shall be as white as snow; though they be red like crimson, they shall be as wool." I decided to *prove* God. I did not challenge the truthfulness of His Word. I wanted to prove Him right and discover what I was overlooking.

This kind of proving is not a self-righteous demand that God justify Himself. It is a humble desire asking God to give instruction and understanding. God invites us to reason with Him. He welcomes our questions. He wants us to learn and understand.

If you are open to learning about God, don't be surprised that you will also learn more about yourself. Understanding truths about God requires clearing the clutter of untruths in your thinking. Perceiving truth requires seeing through a clean window. The cleaner the window, the clearer the perception.

1988–1989 MY BIG GOAL FOR THE YEAR

Every year I set a big goal for myself. In March 1988, I decided that for the next twelve months, my goal would be to understand the prayers that move mountains mentioned in Mark 11:22–23. I asked an elderly pastor friend to pray for me, and he said he would.

As I began my study on prayer, my mind flashed back to 1976 when I was preparing to transfer from UCI to Arkansas. Chuck Schwartz's wife had challenged me to pray as I prepared to leave. It was a memorable moment because she took me aside from an outdoor group meeting. We sat on a concrete bench, and she told me that prayer was the one thing I should never neglect. She encouraged me to always be prayerful. Little did I know at that time that God was speaking to me about prayer.

A PRAYER ANSWERED?

I asked God to help me understand Mark 11:22–23. I wanted to experience the prayers that move mountains and that make miracles happen. I did not want to just talk about it. I wanted to experience it. And now I was faced with the possibility of having cancer. I wondered, *Could this be God's answer to my prayer? Was this my mountain?*

As I said before, I am not satisfied with talking about God and His promises. I want to experience God and His promises. So God was taking me from Bible study *about* prayers that move mountains to the experience of prayers that move mountains.

GREAT INSIGHTS TO REMEMBER

1. A falsehood thought to be true is very difficult to correct.
2. It is possible for atheists and agnostics to become believers.
3. Failure to find answers does not mean there are no answers.
4. The more committed you are to God, the more meaning you have in your life.
5. God invites seekers to reason with Him.
6. Salvation by grace excludes the checklists of efforts to be saved.
7. Subjective truth does not require the ability to prove to others its truth.
8. Your choice is acceptance or rejection of God's personalized message and confirmation to you.
9. You do not have to be a hero in the faith to experience God.
10. God and His Word are testable.
11. To find God, be humble, and keep an open mind to Him.

3
PRAYERS THAT MOVE MOUNTAINS

If ye have faith as a grain of mustard seed, ye shall say unto this mountain, Remove hence to yonder place; and it shall remove; and nothing shall be impossible unto you.
— Matthew 17:20

I prayerfully embarked on my study of prayer with particular interest in Mark 11:22–23 and its promise that requests would be granted to those who believe without doubting. I looked forward to this study because I had offered prayers to God, believing without a hint of doubt, and they were not granted. So my prayer and study were all about understanding why some prayers are not granted in spite of the promise made in Mark 11:22–23.

I am not afraid of God. He is my friend. He loves me. I love

> *I wanted to experience for myself prayers that move mountains. Christ promised this experience to any one who believed.*

Him. I talk to Him all the time about everything. I make many requests. I do not fear asking God questions. In fact, I try to think of the hardest questions that I can ask Him. I ask Him to help me understand verses that appear to contradict real world experiences. I in no way disrespect God in asking these questions. I want to understand. He wants me to understand. He wants everyone to understand and not to be afraid to ask Him any question.

I began my study on prayers that move mountains in March of 1988. They were not a part of my personal experience, and I wanted to find out from God why. I wanted to know how to learn about His promise.

FAITH, BELIEF, AND RIGHTEOUSNESS

You might be reading this book to discover why the answers to your prayers are unpredictable or why your prayers are not answered at all. If you are like I was, you are struggling with the disappointment of prayers that seem not to be answered. You are wondering why some prayers are answered and others are not. You may have even come across questionable news polls claiming that prayerful people sick in the hospital are no more likely to recover than those who never pray.

Disappointments, a lack of explanation, and a lack of understanding make it difficult to sustain the practice of prayer. You can't help but wonder if praying really does any good. And when you are not convinced it does, then you are not motivated to pray. Why bother doing something if there is no benefit? It is difficult to pray when you do not believe that it will make a difference.

The disciples struggled with motivation to pray. Even while they were with Jesus in the Garden of Gethsemane during His greatest hour of crisis, the disciples fell asleep during their prayer meeting. Does this sound like you?

When you doubt whether prayer really is necessary, then it is difficult to pray. You may find that your prayer life becomes active only when you are with others. It becomes nothing more than a practice of public piety for others to see.

This is the way it was for the Jewish leaders. They did not have a relationship with God, as Jesus made clear to them and others (John 8:42–44). But they claimed they did. And they prayed. But Jesus explained to His disciples in Matthew 6:5 that the Jewish leaders at that time were not praying to God. How could they be? They did not even know God. Their religious facade was a pretense of knowing God.

Their prayers were used to make people think that they knew God. Their prayers were a false display of piety to fool people. And for this false display, Jesus said they received their reward. They received the honor and praise of men, not of God, because their prayers were for men, not for God.

Whether you are like the Jewish leaders in Jesus' day or like His disciples in the Garden of Gethsemane, it is possible to learn how to genuinely pray more, for more, and more effectively. I did, and so have others. You can too.

From my study of prayer, I discovered that there are three minimum requirements for prayer, four types of prayers, and four foundational truths of prayer. Understanding these principles of prayer will motivate you to pray more. But my big goal was to understand the prayers that move mountains, and I am eager to share my discovery with you.

Mountain-moving prayers are for miracles that would otherwise not be expected or that would not be explainable as being normal. They are prayers for things that defy natural explanation.

Prayers that move mountains require three minimum criteria: *faith, belief,* and *righteousness. Faith* is revelation from God. *Belief* is our confident acceptance of God's revelation. And *righteousness* is what makes prayer acceptable to God.

FAITH

A year before I was correctly diagnosed with cancer, I had begun my study on prayers that move mountains. At the time, I didn't know *how* God would teach me or even exactly *what* I would discover about prayer. But I knew God wanted me to understand prayer. I knew He would reveal His truth and wisdom about prayer in time. I just needed to ask Him, study His Word, and be patient.

> *The most important thing that opened my eyes to understanding the prayers that move mountains was the phrase "Have faith in God."*

God was in control, and He timed my diagnosis in relation to my study on prayer to make it clear to me that He was answering my prayer.

Just a couple of weeks after setting my goal to understand prayers that move mountains and beginning my study on prayer, I developed symptoms of a "sinus infection." A year later, just one week after my study ended, I was diagnosed with cancer. God answered my prayer. He guided me through Scriptures to understand prayer, and then He took me through the experience of applying the lessons of prayer. I soon realized that this was not a lesson about prayer to talk about prayer. This was a lesson with practical, real-world application. In science, we call this classroom training with lab and field training. I do wonder if I had completed my study sooner, if I would have been diagnosed with cancer sooner.

My study began with Mark 11:22-23. I read this verse many times, studied the words, and pondered the meaning. It says, "And Jesus answering saith unto them, Have faith in God. For verily I say unto you, That whosoever shall say unto this mountain, Be thou removed, and be thou cast into the sea; and shall not doubt in his heart, but shall believe that those things which he saith shall come to pass; he shall have whatsoever he saith."

The most important thing that opened my eyes to understanding the prayers that move mountains was the phrase "Have faith in God." I had read it many times but had overlooked the importance of its meaning with regard to moving mountains with prayer. I do not neglect explaining the meaning of this key ingredient to prayer anymore.

Our pastor had taught the subject of *faith* and had defined it many times. He emphasized how it was not belief. My personal Bible study convinced me that he was right. The Biblical definition of *faith* is very different from the way it is used by most today, even by most Christians. It is commonly accepted to mean belief, but the Bible does not use it this way.

BIBLICAL FAITH

Hebrews 11:1 defines *faith*, saying, "Now faith is the substance of things hoped for, the evidence of things not seen." According to the Bible, faith is revealed information (substance) and confirmed truth (evidence) from God. Because of *revealed information* and *confirmed truth*, understanding God's message is possible (Hebrews 11:3). So Biblical faith is a seeing faith.

Unbelievers know nothing of Biblical faith as it is defined by Hebrews 11:1. Unbelievers cannot distinguish between their

> *Biblical faith is a seeing faith.*

worldly, blind faith and *Biblical*, seeing faith because they have no experience with Biblical faith. To them, worldly faith and Biblical faith are the same. So faith to *them* is *blind belief*. Faith to them is not about knowing something because it is confirmed by revelation from God. They do not have experience with understanding truths revealed from God. For unbelievers, faith is simply blindly believing something to be true.

Unfortunately, many Christians have accepted the unbeliever's definition of *faith* and live in blind belief. They don't have to, but they don't *expect* to believe because of knowing or understanding something, or having a reason to believe something. They just believe with the blind faith of an unbeliever.

The definition of faith has been hijacked. It has been corrupted to mean blind belief. This confuses people and keeps them from understanding truths. But God is not a God of confusion and blindness. He is the God of understanding, light, and vision. He gives sight to the blind and helps the ignorant understand.

In one study session, I was asked to explain the meaning of Second Corinthians 5:7, which says, "For we walk by faith, not by sight." The student sincerely asked why faith was contrasted with sight if faith were not blind. I explained that the Apostle Paul is contrasting physical sight with spiritual sight. He is contrasting the two different ways of seeing and knowing things. He is saying that we rely on *faith*, which is knowledge *spiritually* revealed and confirmed to us from God, for the confidence we have in God's promise of eternal life. We do not rely on *physical* circumstances and rationale of men to determine the promises of God. We rely on spiritual sight to know those things which are spiritually discerned.

Paul is not saying that we should live blindly without understanding of what we believe and do as Christians. Such an interpretation contradicts God's invitation in Isaiah 1:18, where He says, "Come now, and let us reason together, saith the LORD." Defining *faith* as blind belief does not match up with the Biblical definition of *faith* in Hebrews 11:1, which says that faith is the *substance* of things hoped for and the *evidence* of things not seen.

> Faith is revelation that comes from God. It is what you believe in.

According to the Bible's definition of *faith* in Hebrews 11:1, faith is not belief. Faith is *revelation* that comes from God. *Belief* is our acceptance of what God reveals to us. Faith is what we believe in.

Obviously, there is a big difference between just believing in something because you want to and believing in something that you understand. It is this difference that determines whether your prayers will move mountains. Biblical faith moves mountains. Blind faith moves nothing. Biblical faith is revelation from God that you believe in. Blind faith is ignorant belief. I am not saying that people who rely on blind faith are not sincere. But they are sincerely wrong. The world has defined blind faith as belief. The Bible defines faith as revelation of spiritual truths from God that you believe in.

I like describing faith as *revelation from God*. This knowledge is confirmed by the fact that God reveals it. It is the experience of revelation personally delivered by God that confirms the promises believers hope for. It is the revelation direct from God that serves as the evidence for things not seen. Knowledge revealed makes it possible to understand God's truths and promises. A fuller description of faith is to say that it is personalized revelation serving as proof from God to confirm truths that may not have physical verification. The revelation of knowledge is the substance and the evidence of God's message. The revealed knowledge is the thing hoped for that is not physically discernible. This means Biblical faith is *revelation from God*. By revelation (faith) from God we know His promises and truths. By revelation we are convicted of our sins. Salvation is by revelation of God's promise, not by the Law of works. Using the Biblical definition of faith gives tremendous insight into Scriptural statements.

ELIJAH'S PRAYER FOR FIRE FROM HEAVEN

Is there an example in the Bible of such faith? Yes. Elijah was one of God's prophets, and he moved a mountain with his prayers.

During a contest with 400 priests of Baal, Elijah called fire down from heaven. This was definitely a mountain-moving prayer that produced a miracle. In First Kings 18:36, Elijah's prayer to God reveals how he was able to do this. It says, "And it came to pass at the time of the offering of the evening sacrifice, that Elijah the prophet came near, and said, LORD God of Abraham, Isaac, and of Israel, let it be known this day that thou art God in Israel, and that I am thy servant, and that I have done all these things at thy word." Elijah said that everything he did was according to the Word of God. Elijah did not have written instructions in a scroll from God about his contest. So how did he know what to do? Biblical faith, revelation from God. God had revealed to Elijah what to do. Elijah believed and prayed, and fire came down out of heaven.

By faith, Elijah knew what God wanted him to do. His prayer was according to God's instructions, spiritually discerned instructions revealed to him. This is *seeing* faith from God. This is faith that gives understanding.

Elijah did not pray to tell God what to do. He did not ask God to help him win the contest against the priests of Baal. God told Elijah what to do. This is a different kind of prayer than what I see commonly practiced today.

In my follow-up study about Elijah, I read James 5:17, which says, "Elias [Elijah] was a man subject to like passions as we are, and he prayed earnestly that it might not rain: and it rained not on the earth by the space of three years and six months." Elijah was able to pray for miracles such as making the rain stop and start. He did miraculous things through prayer, and yet he was a "man subject to like passions as we are." This means he was just an ordinary man like the rest of us. Elijah was an ordinary man who experienced extraordinary things. James 5:17 gives us hope of being like him.

As stated before, Elijah prayed because God told him what to do. Elijah did not tell God what to do. This is the kind of prayer that moves mountains. It is prayer *because* of faith (revelation).

A QUIET VOICE

How obvious is this revealed knowledge from God? From my personal experience and observation of others' experiences, it is often like a quiet voice in your thoughts. Elijah had this experience. First Kings 19:11–13 describes an interesting demonstration from God to teach Elijah about quiet revelation. "And he said, Go forth, and stand upon the mount before the LORD. And, behold, the LORD passed by, and a great and strong wind rent the mountains, and brake in pieces the rocks before the LORD; but the LORD was not in the wind: and after the wind an earthquake; but the LORD was not in the earthquake: And after the earthquake a fire; but the LORD was not in the fire: and after the fire a still small voice. And it was so, when Elijah heard it, that he wrapped his face in his mantle, and went out, and stood in the entering in of the cave. And, behold, there came a voice unto him, and said, What doest thou here, Elijah?"

God was teaching Elijah to expect revelation from Him as a quiet voice, not as a loud announcement. This is how faith is experienced. It is personalized, spiritually discerned instruction from God. To hear the voice of God requires careful listening on our part. It requires a humility and sense of dependence on God to help us discern His voice. It requires thoughtfulness and careful mental testing of the message to determine if it is from God.

The experience in the early church in Antioch illustrates how the voice of God is discerned. Acts 13:2–3 says, "As they ministered to the Lord, and fasted, the Holy Ghost said, Separate me Barnabas and Saul for the work whereunto I have called them. And when they had fasted and prayed, and laid their hands on them, they sent them away." How did the Holy Ghost speak to the elders of the church? By faith. God's will was revealed to them. Notice that they were ministering to the Lord, fasting, and praying when the Holy Ghost spoke to them. This tells us that they were listening very carefully for the "still, small voice" of God.

My church adopted the practice of listening for the voice of God. For example, rather than vote for church decisions, we ask for members to prayerfully indicate what the Spirit of God is revealing to them. Collectively, we confirm the quiet voice of God. Proverbs 11:14 reinforces our practice, saying, "… in the multitude of counsellors there is safety."

KNOWING

How do we *know* that Jesus is more than a man? How do we *know* that Jesus is the Son of God? How do we *know* that we are sinners? How do we *know* that Jesus is the Savior? How do we *know* that God promises eternal life to believers? Even if there were no physical evidences for these truths, we know these things, and more, because God reveals these truths to us. This revelation is faith. And it is this *revelation of truth* from God that confirms truth to us. And thus *faith is spiritually discerned knowledge confirmed by personalized revelation from God.*

Jesus explained this experience of knowing in Matthew 16:16–17, which says, "And Simon Peter answered and said, Thou art the Christ, the Son of the living God. And Jesus answered and said unto him, Blessed art thou, Simon Barjona: for flesh and blood hath not revealed it unto thee, but my Father which is in heaven." Faith is from God, not from the wisdom and teaching of people.

The revelation of knowledge from God is the substance of things hoped for because it is truth personally revealed by God, who cannot lie. Titus 1:2 says, "In hope of eternal life, which God, that cannot lie, promised before the world began." And Hebrews 6:18 says, "That by two immutable things, in which [it was] impossible for God to lie, we might have a strong consolation, who have fled for refuge to lay hold upon the hope set before us."

> *Faith is spiritually discerned knowledge revealed by God and personally confirmed by Him.*

Likewise, the revelation from God is evidence of truth because God personally reveals the knowledge to us. This personalization of knowledge revealed directly from God is confirmed evidence that His message is true. Ultimately, this makes God the evidence for truth revealed because He is the one revealing the message.

UNDERSTANDING

Because faith is revealed knowledge from God, it is possible to *understand* God's truths. Hebrews 11:3 explains, "Through faith we understand that the worlds were framed by the word of God, so that things which are seen were not made of things which do appear." Because of revelation from God, we are able to understand the truth of God's involvement in creating all things. No one was present at the start of creation. But through faith, which is *by means of revelation*, God confirms what He did. This revelation is evidence direct from God to confirm to us what He did. And through discoveries of physical laws and properties of matter in creation, we now have physical evidence to support what has been previously only spiritually discerned.

Paul says that by faith Christians understand their personal roles in their churches. He says in Romans 12:3, "… God hath dealt to every man the measure of faith." This means that God reveals knowledge to church members what they should be doing in His churches. Everyone has a God-given role to fulfill.

By faith, believers are given information from God on how to fulfill their roles in the church. First Corinthians 12:27 says, "Now ye are the body of Christ, and members in particular." A church is put together like a body. Of course, every body needs a head to do the thinking, and Christ assumes that obvious position. He is the head of every church body.

I was amazed when I heard that the family of God and the church of God were two different things. I had to study that for myself very carefully and pray for understanding. And sure enough, I discovered that the Bible's definition of *the church* is different from the world's definition. And like the redefining of *faith*, the redefining of the word *church* hinders one from fully understanding God's will.

I discovered that all believers are in the family of God, but not all believers are in the church of God. The family of God includes everyone who believes and has eternal life. The church is a local group of baptized believers who work with one another and coordinate with other churches to do God's work.

I came across a book during my study on the church by Dr. Earl Radmacher, who served as the Western Seminary president for twenty-five years. He said the Bible and the early church knew nothing of a universal, invisible church. He went on to explain how and why the word *church* was redefined. After studying every verse in the Bible referencing the words *church* and *churches*, I came to the same conclusion. Once again, a word in the Bible had been redefined.

The meaning of the word *church* is obvious in the Bible. When

I read Acts and Revelation, I read about the church at Jerusalem, the church at Ephesus, the church at Antioch, the church at Thyatira, the church at Sardis, and so forth. And each of the letters in the New Testament is written to a church, and references are made to other churches.

There are only a few verses which refer to the collection of churches. Just as all humans come from Adam, yet all are individuals, likewise, every church comes from the original church in Jerusalem, yet each is an individual church. Speaking about a church or the church is like speaking of a human being. It is understood that the human being is a special creation of God designed in the image of God and is different from the frog, the dog, the monkey, and so on. Likewise, the church is a body of believers who make a covenant with each other to work together to do God's work God's way as a local church of baptized believers. Just as the human being is not a universal, invisible human, the church is not a universal, invisible body of believers.

Ephesians 5:23 generically refers to the church, the husband, and the wife, saying, "For the husband is the head of the wife, even as Christ is the head of the church: and he is the saviour of the body." Obviously, no one confuses husband and wife with a universal, invisible husband and a universal, invisible wife. So it is not appropriate to confuse the church with a universal, invisible church. The family of God includes all believers, and the church of God includes all baptized believers in their respective local churches.

As a seeker, I did not know what the word *church* meant in the Bible. In fact, I had told people that I did not need to attend a local, physical church because I was already in the church (universal, invisible) as a believer. My confusion hindered my spiritual growth and insights into what God wanted me to do. By faith, study of the Bible, and good teaching, I finally came to understand my need for a local church home and my role in my church.

Biblical faith and a Biblical church were essential to me for understanding correctly what kind of prayers move mountains.

FAITH IS PERSONALIZED REVELATION

Faith is not a physical revelation like experimenting in a laboratory or reading the Bible. It is spiritual revelation from God.

Nonetheless, in both cases, physical and spiritual, God reveals truth about Himself. When we study the Bible or the physical creation, we are discovering more about God. When we study the physical, tangible world, God reveals a great deal to us. But faith is knowledge given to us directly and personally by God. It is spiritually discerned knowledge that is not subject to examination outside of us except by the Bible.

> *Faith is subjective truth rather than objective truth.*

Faith is *subjective* truth rather than *objective* truth. It is truth that God reveals and confirms to each of us individually. At best, we can compare notes with others who have faith and realize that we have the same message from God. But we cannot examine the revelation mechanism and knowledge in people to determine if they were telling the truth.

Understanding faith as subjective truth helps us to understand the meaning of Romans 1:17, which says, "For therein is the righteousness of God revealed from faith to faith: as it is written, The just shall live by faith." From one person's faith to another's, God's message of salvation (the Gospel) is the same. We are sinners and are facing God's judgment. Salvation from judgment must be by the mercy and grace of God because there is nothing we can do to pay the debt we owe for our sins. Through Jesus Christ, everyone who believes in Him receives the promise of God's mercy and grace. This message is understood by those having faith, and it is consistent with the message revealed in the Bible.

The choice to accept or reject God's personalized message to you is your personal choice. The fact that God's message to you is personalized means that it does not rely on someone else to confirm it for you. Likewise, what God reveals to you is true, whether anyone else believes it or not. You do not have to prove your faith (God's personalized revelation to you) to anyone to make it true. It is God's message to you. And it is your responsibility to believe it, regardless of what others believe.

When I came to realize that faith is revelation from God that is confirmed personally by God, I could see why sharing the Gospel with people often produces a strong reaction (conviction). When people hear the Gospel message, God confirms to them personally that Christ is inviting them to accept His gift of salvation.

The revelation from God (called faith) is *what* is believed. To be without revelation and understanding from God is to be faithless.

On one occasion, after I shared the Gospel with a college student, she broke down in tears. She said that God was definitely confirming in her that she was in need of His mercy and grace. I asked her why she was crying. She said that even though she knew God was talking to her by faith, she had to reject Him because her boyfriend would not approve of her becoming a Christian. No wonder she broke down! She was choosing to go to hell for her boyfriend. That was crazy!

Have you experienced faith from God? Has God ever revealed and confirmed to you that sin in your life condemns you? Has God ever revealed and confirmed to you that there is nothing you can do to save yourself from condemnation? Has God ever revealed and confirmed to you that He alone must save you? Has God ever revealed and confirmed to you that He wants to save you? I have no doubt that He has. The real question is were you and are you listening and willing to accept His message?

You may recall in the previous chapter I explained that according to Romans 1:16–23 God reveals Himself to everyone. Verse 19 says, "Because that which may be known of God is manifest in them; for God hath shewed it unto them." But some reject God's revelation of Himself. Verse 21 says, "Because that, when they knew God, they glorified him not as God, neither were thankful; but became vain in their imaginations, and their foolish heart was darkened." This explains the reason you are uncertain about God. You have already rejected Him. Now you have to pray and seek Him again. But remember to do it with humility and be careful to listen for that quiet voice.

God loves you and initiates the search. You search for Him only because He is revealing Himself to you. He is giving you hope of finding a solution. Jesus came to seek and to save that which was lost.

As an agnostic searching for God, before I made my atheism official, I prayed for His help. I wasn't convinced that He was there, so I asked Him to reveal Himself to me and to help me understand if He were real and, if so, what He expected of me. I asked Him to give me something to believe in. If you are sincere and listening carefully, He will help you return to His light and truth. This is His desire, and He was willing to die to make it possible for you to know Him.

Romans 10:17 says, "So then faith [cometh] by hearing, and hearing by the word of God." When you hear the Word of God taught, God personalizes that message by confirming it with His assurance that it is true. This shows that *faith is not merely knowledge*. When someone shares God's message with you, you have knowledge. This is not faith. But when God *reveals* and confirms that knowledge personally to you, you receive faith.

Faith is God's message revealed to you personally. Rather than just another message being heard, it is a message that is confirmed personally and directly by revelation from God. Rejecting revelation from God is personal rejection of Him.

FAITH OR BELIEF?

When I focused on Jesus saying *have faith in God*, I realized the problem I was having in understanding Mark 11:22–23. When *faith* is thought of as *belief*, then people think all they have to do is believe in what *they ask for* in order to move mountains. This is blind belief because they believe what *they* want, not what *God* wants. This kind of faith is belief in what they want, not what God reveals.

Faith is not the act of believing. It is revelation from God of what He wants us to believe and pray for.

They think that by believing a miracle will happen, it will happen. They name and claim it. They believe with all their hearts and cast out all doubts from their minds. And then ... nothing happens. Their prayers are not granted. I know this kind of prayer from personal experience. It is very disappointing.

What is the problem? They believed without faith. They believed without the understanding that comes with revealed knowledge. *Faith is not the act of believing.* It is revelation from God of what He wants us to believe and pray for.

Because faith is confused with believing, many believers discredit themselves when their claims are contradicted by reality. They believe that something will happen, but it does not.

How many people have been disappointed and disillusioned over many failed claims and experiences of believing that something will happen that never happens? No wonder people quit believing. Some abandon the faith altogether. Others resign themselves to believing anyway but with a defeated attitude and little hope of receiving an answer. Others burden themselves with self-rebuke, thinking they did not believe enough, they were not good enough, or they were deceived by the devil. Still others blame God for not listening to their sincere prayers, or they decide that the Bible and its promises are not true. Sadly, "blind faith" has caused a spiritual crisis in many sincere believers' lives.

Tragically, charlatans have come along and preyed on those desperately wanting to believe but who do not understand Biblical faith. These false prophets take advantage of sincere believers and mislead them with fakery and false claims of miracles.

During my first year of being involved with Christian ministries, I was introduced to many questionable experiences. Friends were claiming to speak in unknown languages; others were holding communion services in their dorm rooms; and still others were attending healing services. They were all sincere. They were all great Christian friends. But sincerity does not make you knowledgeable and wise.

Colleen and I went to a healing service in Chino, California. Betty Baxter was the healer. Carl, a high school friend of mine, joined us because he had a deformed finger he wanted healed. I had back problems I wanted fixed. Colleen went because I asked her to. Baxter was "slaying people in the spirit," which involved pushing people on their foreheads, and then they would fall backward. Someone was behind them to catch and lower them to the floor.

Carl and I both fell to the floor because that is what everyone else did, but it turned out that Colleen never did. She was waiting to be knocked out by the Spirit, and it did not happen. Baxter pushed her head three times, each time harder. But Colleen did not fall.

We heard nothing about anyone being healed that evening. But we believed that God could and would heal us. I was determined not to allow unbelief on my part to prevent my healing. In spite of believing without doubt in our minds, Carl and I were not healed. But in the newspaper the next day, there was a story about a man in a wheelchair who walked after Baxter healed him. We did not see that man while we were there.

Second Corinthians 11:13–15 says of charlatans, "For such are false apostles, deceitful workers, transforming themselves into the apostles of Christ. And no marvel; for Satan himself is transformed into an angel of light. Therefore it is no great thing if his ministers also be transformed as the ministers of righteousness; whose end shall be according to their works." These false prophets corrupt the reputation of Christ and His followers, and they turn many sincere believers and seekers into doubters.

Mark 11:22–23 and its promise have been a source of misery for many people. The problem is not with the promise and not with God. The problem is with misunderstanding the meaning of *faith*. Believers can protect themselves from charlatans and from disappointment with their prayer lives by understanding that faith is not belief.

Prayers that move mountains often require that God first *reveal* to us the mountain to be moved. This revelation is faith. In this case, God reveals His will before we pray. If you believe what God first reveals and confirms to you (faith), it will come to pass, and nothing can prevent it. This is the promise made by Jesus in Mark 11:22–23. Alternatively, if you make your request without revelation from God first, there is no guarantee that God will do what you ask. For example, you can ask God to heal you, and if it be God's will, healing will take place. In the first case, God first reveals what He wants. In the second case, you first make your request.

FAITH AS A MUSTARD SEED

What does it mean to have faith as a mustard seed? It is not the quantity of knowledge revealed to us that moves mountains. If we understand what God wants us to believe and to pray for, it will be done. This personal revelation from God is all we need to know. We do not need deep understanding. We do not need to know how He does it. We do not need to know why He wants it done. We need only to know what He wants us to believe and pray for. It is that simple.

Faith as a grain of mustard seed means that you need only to know what God wants you to believe and pray for.

Jesus explained the sufficiency of a little revelation in Luke 17:6, which says, "And the Lord said, If ye had faith as a grain of mustard seed, ye might say unto this sycamine tree, Be thou plucked up by the root, and be thou planted in the sea; and it should obey you." This was Jesus' answer to His disciples' request that Jesus increase their faith (understanding revealed from God). He had just told them to forgive others as often as they ask to be forgiven. They struggled to understand why and how to do that. So they asked Jesus to increase their understanding. This is when Jesus told them having faith as a grain of mustard seed is all they needed. In other words, they were not lacking in faith. They understood enough to forgive others.

Jesus explained that fulfilling God's will in their lives did not require deep understanding. It required only that they believe what had been revealed to them. Jesus was giving them sufficient explanation and understanding. They were given enough faith (revelation). They just needed to believe it and do it.

On another occasion, the disciples asked why they could not heal a man from self-destructive behavior. Matthew 17:14–21 records the event and conversation, saying, "And when they were come to the multitude, there came to him a certain man, kneeling down to him, and saying, Lord, have mercy on my son: for he is lunatick, and sore vexed: for ofttimes he falleth into the fire, and oft into the water. And I brought him to thy disciples, and they could not cure him. Then Jesus answered and said, O faithless and perverse generation, how long shall I be with you? how long shall I suffer you? bring him hither to me. And Jesus rebuked the devil; and he departed out of him: and the child was cured from that very hour. Then came the disciples to Jesus apart, and said, Why could not we cast him out? And Jesus said unto them, Because of your unbelief: for verily I say unto you, If ye have faith as a grain of mustard seed, ye shall say unto this mountain, Remove hence to yonder place; and it shall remove; and nothing shall be impossible unto you. Howbeit this kind goeth not out but by prayer and fasting."

I find this story very interesting because the disciples obviously believed enough to try to help the man's son. Being around Jesus and believing in Him, they no doubt believed in God. They believed that God had the power to heal. They believed that God would respond to their request to heal the man's son. And yet, Jesus told them that their problem was unbelief.

This story sounds like many stories of today. People believe and they pray, but nothing happens. This was my experience. So I asked the Lord to teach me. This is the same question the disciples asked Jesus. I would venture to say many people ask the same question after praying and believing for something that does not happen. Jesus said the problem is because of unbelief.

Jesus explained to the disciples that they were not lacking in faith. They had enough faith to help the man's son because faith as small as a grain of mustard seed is sufficient to move mountains. That is to say, they had enough understanding of what God wanted to do for the man's son and what He required of the disciples. With just the tiniest bit of revealed understanding (faith), mountains can be moved. Their problem was unbelief. So what is it that they did not believe?

They failed to believe what God had revealed to them. What was that? Jesus told them that some miracles, such as healing the man's son, required prayer and fasting. This is what they did not believe. They did not think that prayer *and* fasting were necessary. They probably thought prayer was sufficient. But Jesus said fasting was required in this case. They did not believe it prior to His telling them. But why not?

I believe they did not believe the revelation to fast was from God and therefore dismissed it. I know from personal experience and from listening to others that thoughts are sometimes not recognized as being from God and are dismissed as unimportant, especially if it involves inconvenience such as fasting. This is the challenge of discerning the quiet voice of God from thoughts that normally come to your mind.

Can God's quiet voice be distinguished from normal thoughts? Yes, with experience and study of the Bible to train your thoughts, you can be more confident in listening for God's voice. Hebrews 5:14 explains, "But strong meat belongeth to them that are of full age, even those who by reason of use have their senses exercised to discern both good and evil." By means of study in God's Word and through personal experience, it is possible to exercise your senses to discern God's quiet voice from other thoughts.

It is apparent that God had revealed to the disciples that they should pray and fast. They had to have known this was required. Otherwise, Jesus would not have rebuked them for unbelief. Because of unbelief, they were not praying *and* fasting.

Why did God require prayer and fasting? Jesus did not explain the reason to the disciples. He simply said that knowing to do so was sufficient. Having faith as a grain of mustard seed is all that is needed to move mountains. It is not knowing why you should do something or how much you know that makes your prayers effective. You need only to know what mountain God wants you to pray for.

THE IMPORTANCE OF FAITH

How important is it to learn how to live by faith? Hebrews 11:6 explains, "But without faith it is impossible to please him: for he that cometh to God must believe that he is, and that he is a rewarder of them that diligently seek him." Without faith, you do not know what to believe. You do not know how to live for God. If you are seeking to please God, you need to seek understanding. You need to ask God for faith. Understanding the role of faith was the most important thing I learned from my study of Mark 11:22–23.

Paul takes the importance of faith a step further, saying in Romans 14:23, "And he that doubteth is damned if he eat, because he eateth not of faith: for whatsoever is not of faith is sin." If we have doubt about doing something, but we do it anyway, then we are doing it without understanding and confirmation from God that it is His will.

Does this mean that we should not pray or do anything without explicit revelation from God to direct every activity, thought, and word in our lives? No.

God does not reveal what to do for every detail of your life. First Corinthians 10:33 says, "Whether therefore ye eat, or drink, or whatsoever ye do, do all to the glory of God." Live for God, and do everything for Him. This is a good general rule that covers everything. We should live every moment of our lives for God. When God does have something in particular for you to pray for or for you to do, He will reveal it to you. Otherwise, the admonition to live for Him is sufficient.

How often can you expect Him to reveal details? That all depends on His will and purpose for your life. But it is not important to know how often. It is more important to listen for His voice and respond when He does reveal details to you.

FAITH AND THE BIBLE

The Bible and faith work together. Both are revelations from God, and both reveal God's Word, His truths, His promises, and His will. For example, the Bible says in Romans 3:23, "For all have sinned, and come short of the glory of God." This truth revealed in the Bible is confirmed by faith, which is *spiritually confirmed knowledge revealed from God*. Likewise, the solution to our sin problem is revealed in the Bible. Galatians 3:22 says, "But the scripture hath concluded all under sin, that the promise by faith of Jesus Christ might be given to them that believe." This Biblical truth is confirmed by faith.

Because the Bible and faith are both from God, they will never contradict each other. This means that our knowledge of the Bible can help us distinguish between God's quiet voice and our own thoughts. We should always test the thoughts we have to determine if they contradict the Bible.

PRAYERS OF THE RIGHTEOUS AVAIL MUCH

Recall the early church receiving instruction from the Holy Ghost in Acts 13:2–3? Those who heard the Holy Ghost were those praying, fasting, and ministering to the Lord. They were listening carefully to the quiet voice of God. God does not intend to shout and make a lot of noise. He reveals His will quietly and personally. Those who discern His instructions are blessed with His revelations.

How do we reach a point of maturity to spiritually discern

God's quiet voice? By following the example of those who have discerned His will. In the case of the early church mentioned in Acts 13, they were praying and fasting. In the case of the disciples failing to heal a man's son from self-destructive behavior, Jesus said, "… this kind goeth not out but by prayer and fasting." This indicates that some things can be done with just prayer and others are done with prayer and fasting. How can you know when fasting is required and when it is not? Listen to the quiet voice of God.

James 5:16 gives us helpful instruction about prayers that avail much, saying, "Confess your faults one to another, and pray one for another, that ye may be healed. The effectual fervent prayer of a righteous man availeth much." Prayers that avail much are prayers that are granted by God. Elijah's prayers availed much. Jesus' prayers availed much. Likewise, Paul's prayers, and Peter's, and many others' prayers were granted. Finding out how to pray like Christ and these men will help us discern what God requires of us in order to avail in our prayers.

> *Prayer is about seeking God's will to be done, not telling Him what to do.*

As I studied and meditated on these verses, I was reminded that Elijah did not tell God what to do. He did what God told him to do. This is a very important insight into prayer that avails much. This shows humility and dependency on the part of Elijah. What made it possible for him to have these attitudes?

James says that the "effectual fervent prayer of a righteous man availeth much." Elijah must have been a righteous man. And anyone who wants to pray prayers that avail much and move mountains must be righteous.

What does it mean to be righteous? I find it very interesting that there are two ways to think about righteousness. There is the nature of righteousness, which refers to what you are. And there is the thought and behavior of righteousness. This is the righteousness you do.

God is righteous by nature. Righteousness is what God is. Psalm 11:7 says, "For the righteous LORD loveth righteousness; his countenance doth behold the upright." The quality of righteousness describes the nature of God. He is not righteous because of what He does. He is righteous because of what He is. God does righteous things because He is righteous.

Jeremiah 9:24 says, "But let him that glorieth glory in this, that he understandeth and knoweth me, that I am the LORD which exercise lovingkindness, judgment, and righteousness, in the earth: for in these things I delight, saith the LORD." So then God is righteous by nature and by what He does.

Distinguishing between God's nature and God's deeds helped me resolve the confusion that many people have about calling someone righteous. There are Bible verses that refer to people as being unrighteous and righteous. Romans 3:10 says, "As it is written, There is none righteous, no, not one." And of course, James 5:16 says, "The effectual fervent prayer of a righteous man availeth much." If no one is righteous, then how can Elijah or anyone else be called righteous? Being able to distinguish between the nature of righteousness and the deeds of righteousness is essential to understanding the answer to this question.

Distinguishing between God's nature and God's deeds helped me resolve the confusion that many people have about calling someone righteous.

Romans 3:22 explains that "Even the righteousness of God which is by faith of Jesus Christ unto all and upon all them that believe: for there is no difference." By faith (revelation of promise), the righteousness of God is given to believers. This means that those who believe the message and promise revealed from God about salvation are given the righteousness of God. They are given a righteous nature. This makes sense because there is only one standard of righteousness in creation. So to be made righteous requires being made with the righteousness of God. This is the reason Romans 3:10 says that there is none righteous. Everyone must depend on God to be made righteous.

The alternative is to try to be righteous on your own. The Bible calls these efforts *works*. Titus 3:5 explains that attempts to be righteous by works will fail, saying, "Not by works of righteousness which we have done, but according to his mercy he saved us, by the washing of regeneration, and renewing of the Holy Ghost." Being made righteous by regeneration and renewing is a miracle. This is what it means to be saved. And this salvation is by the mercy and grace of God because He does the work. Believers simply benefit from the promise and work that God does.

Romans 4:5 says that righteousness must come by faith. "But to him that worketh not, but believeth on him that justifieth the ungodly, his faith is counted for righteousness." Those who rely on the promise of God (faith) rather than on their own works are counted in God's eyes as righteous. This righteousness is the *nature* of being righteous. And Second Corinthians 5:21 tells us that righteousness comes by faith (revealed promise of God). It says, "… that we might be made the righteousness of God in him." Trying to be righteous any other way will not succeed in reaching the standard of God's righteousness.

With this insight about righteousness, we understand why the prayers of *believers* avail much. This is the meaning of "the effectual fervent prayer of a righteous man" in James 5:16.

This raised a question in my mind. Does this mean that God

does not hear the prayers of the unrighteous? They are not righteous prior to believing in God's message and promise. So then how can they be made righteous if God does not hear their prayers? They simply believe, and then they pray prayers that God will hear. They pray prayers that avail because they believe and are changed by God.

But what about the prayers of the unrighteous (lost sinners) that lead them eventually to salvation? For example, I asked God to help me find Him. He did. My prayers requesting that He show Himself to me were not granted in the way I imagined, but He did reveal His message and promise to me so I could believe. I was lost. I prayed. God heard my prayers and granted them.

Taking into consideration the granting of prayers of the unrighteous, I realized that when James 5:17 says the prayers of the righteous avail much, this does not mean the prayers of the unrighteous are not heard. After all, God is omniscient. How could He know everything if He does not hear the prayers of the lost?

God hears the prayers of the unrighteous crying out for salvation, and He answers those prayers. This undoubtedly is the one prayer that God loves to hear the most. When a repentant sinner calls out for His mercy and grace, He is more than ready to answer.

> God hears the prayers of the unrighteous crying out for salvation, and He answers those prayers.

God promises to grant the prayers of those who cry out to Him for salvation. Romans 10:13 says, "For whosoever shall call upon the name of the Lord shall be saved." There is no question about the answer one receives to this prayer. The answer is guaranteed, and it is immediate. Jesus says in John 5:24, "Verily, verily, I say unto you, He that heareth my word, and believeth on him that sent me, hath everlasting life, and shall not come into condemnation;

but is passed from death unto life." This means that the moment someone believes in Jesus Christ and His message, he instantly receives eternal life and is delivered from eternal death.

Once we are saved, we are instantly changed. We are miraculously made righteous. Our sins are forgiven, and our spirits are born again. This change takes place inside us spiritually. Because we're made righteous in our spirits, we are called righteous. We are righteous in God's eyes. And because we are righteous, our prayers are effective.

> *It is because of being made righteous inwardly that we are called righteous.*

Being saved and made righteous does not change our physical bodies right away. That comes later. We must wait for the complete redemption Paul speaks of in Romans 8:23, which says, "And not only [they], but ourselves also, which have the firstfruits of the Spirit, even we ourselves groan within ourselves, waiting for the adoption, [to wit], the redemption of our body."

Your body is obviously not born again. This is the reason, as a believer, you struggle with temptations to sin. Physically, which includes the thoughts and emotions you are aware of, you are the same as you were before you were saved. Jesus explained to Nicodemus in John 3:6, "That which is born of the flesh is flesh; and that which is born of the Spirit is spirit." The spirit was born again and made righteous. This is the inward man Paul speaks about in Romans 7:22, which says, "For I delight in the law of God after the inward man." But the outward man, which is the body of flesh, is not born again. Paul said of it in Romans 7:18, "For I know that in me (that is, in my flesh,) dwelleth no good thing: for to will is present with me; but [how] to perform that which is good I find not."

The description of born-again believers in Romans 7:15–25

explains why Christians can be born again and made righteous but still struggle with the presence of sinful thoughts and behavior.

The bodies of born-again Christians remain unrighteous until after they die. Their bodies still have the old sin nature and are in conflict with their spirits within. Paul makes it sound like a tug-o-war in Romans 7:15, saying, "For that which I do I allow not: for what I would, that do I not; but what I hate, that do I."

Prayers that avail much require that a person be *made* righteous *spiritually* and *contend* with their *bodies* to think and behave righteously. This is a struggle that even the Apostle Paul despaired of, saying in Romans 7:24, "O wretched man that I am! who shall deliver me from the body of this death?" Nonetheless, Paul said in First Corinthians 9:27 that he was able to bring his body under subjection. It was a daily fight to do so because his body was not changed.

It is our flesh, not our born-again spirits that we must contend with for a good prayer life. The flesh is stubborn and delights in sin. And when we yield to the flesh rather than to the spirit, we offend God. That hurts our prayer life and makes it difficult to hear the quiet voice of God.

Fortunately, God has secured us in His promise of righteousness and eternal life by the miracle of new birth in the inward man. This is the work He did. Regardless of what the outward man does, the inward man is always doing right. It is not possible for finite people to undo the work of an infinite God. But yielding to the flesh will rob us of blessings such as prayers that avail much.

If you want to enjoy prayers that avail much, you need to believe in God's promise and contend with the impulses of unrighteousness in your flesh. This will help you understand and experience success in prayer.

MOVING YOUR MOST IMPORTANT MOUNTAIN

As mentioned earlier, prayer involves three minimal requirements: faith, belief, and righteousness. Lacking any one of these in your prayers will result in praying amiss. If your prayers are not being granted, it means that you lack faith, belief, or righteousness.

Faith is revelation from God. Because this revelation is directly from God, it serves to confirm spiritually discerned knowledge and makes it possible to understand what and how to pray. *Belief* is accepting and trusting the message and promise of God that is revealed. *Righteousness* is miraculously given by God to believers and is manifested in the lives of those desiring to please God.

I hope it is clear that prayers that avail much are not prayers of our own skill and power. They are prayers of understanding and humility. They are prayers of understanding that God is credited with the power, the glory, and the honor of granted prayers. They are prayers of understanding that we depend on God for everything. Romans 8:26 reminds us, "Likewise the Spirit also helpeth our infirmities: for we know not what we should pray for as we ought: but the Spirit itself maketh intercession for us with groanings which cannot be uttered."

Becoming a Christian and living like a Christian are by the grace of God. Grace is necessary because we do not possess the ability to do as we should. We must depend on God to help us at all times.

Consider the salvation experience. Ephesians 2:8–9 says, "For by grace are ye saved through faith; and that not of yourselves: it is the gift of God: Not of works, lest any man should boast." Faith is the revelation of God that shows us how helpless we are to save ourselves. It is impossible for us to do anything to save ourselves. We need God to save us. He alone must do all the work necessary to save us from sin and condemnation.

Paul raises important questions about salvation and works in

Romans 3:27–28, asking, "Where is boasting then? It is excluded. By what law? of works? Nay: but by the law of faith. Therefore we conclude that a man is justified by faith without the deeds of the law." If individuals could claim that they did something good enough to gain God's favor, they would have accomplished something to boast about. But there is no boasting involved in salvation. The Law is not of faith (revealed *promise* of God's work to save). The Law condemns us.

If you are thinking that keeping the Law is impossible, you are right. The Law was given to convince unbelievers that they are not acceptable in God's eyes, whereas faith shows that only believers are acceptable, The Law shows what you must do (or can't do). Faith shows what only God can do.

Romans 11:6 states plainly that Law and grace are *mutually exclusive*. "And if by grace, then is it no more of works: otherwise grace is no more grace. But if it be of works, then is it no more grace: otherwise work is no more work." Law and grace cannot be mixed and combined in any way. Salvation must be all by grace without any works.

The grace of God is what makes salvation free to us. Paul explains in Romans 3:24, "Being justified freely by his grace through the redemption that is in Christ Jesus." Grace is necessary because we are all sinners. We cannot do anything good enough to deserve salvation. Instead, we deserve just the opposite.

In my study of the Bible, I discovered that being a sinner disqualifies us from being able to offer anything that would be acceptable to God. No matter how good we might be, we can never be good enough to be worthy of salvation. This is true for everyone, without exception. Paul describes man's condition in Romans 3:23, saying, "For all have sinned, and come short of the glory of God."

I know some are offended when told that they are sinners. But it is true. It never bothered me to be told that I was a sinner because I knew I was. Everyone is a sinner. No one is exempt but God. No one is righteous. This is the reason God must offer salvation to us as a free gift. We do not deserve it, and we cannot earn it. We cannot even begin to show some worthiness of salvation because we are not worthy, no matter how hard we try to be.

Romans 3:20 says, "Therefore by the deeds of the law there shall no flesh be justified in his sight: for by the law is the knowledge of sin." Some think the Ten Commandments were given to show us how to be righteous and what to do to be good enough to go to heaven. But this thinking is the opposite of what God intended to accomplish with the Law.

First Timothy 1:9–10 explains, "Knowing this, that the law is not made for a righteous man, but for the lawless and disobedient, for the ungodly and for sinners, for unholy and profane, for murderers of fathers and murderers of mothers, for manslayers, For whoremongers, for them that defile themselves with mankind, for menstealers, for liars, for perjured persons, and if there be any other thing that is contrary to sound doctrine." Simply put, the Law was given to convince us that we are not righteous. We are sinners.

Why do we need the Law? We need it to expose our unrighteousness and convince us that we are sinners. Many of us deny that we are sinners. Many more deny that we are bad enough to be rejected by God. So God gave us the Law to show us that we are not good enough to be acceptable to Him and that we need His help. We need His mercy and grace.

Why does a righteous man not need the Law? Because a righteous man already keeps the Law. He keeps the righteousness of the Law because he is righteous. But if we are all sinners, how do we become righteous? Believe in Jesus Christ. In John 11:25, "Jesus said ..., I am the resurrection, and the life: he that believeth in me, though he were dead, yet shall he live."

The mountain of sin and condemnation is the first mountain needing to be moved. Everyone needs to be born again and experience a nature change. This is a miracle. Has it happened in your life yet?

During a conversation with a Pharisee recorded in John 3:3–7, Jesus said, "... Verily, verily, I say unto thee, Except a man be born again, he cannot see the kingdom of God. Nicodemus saith unto him, How can a man be born when he is old? can he enter the second time into his mother's womb, and be born? Jesus answered, Verily, verily, I say unto thee, Except a man be born of water and of the Spirit, he cannot enter into the kingdom of God. That which is born of the flesh is flesh; and that which is born of the Spirit is spirit. Marvel not that I said unto thee, Ye must be born again."

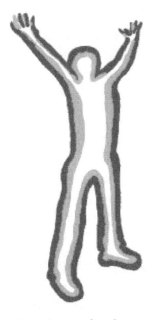

Man has a body, a soul, and a spirit. (First Thessalonians 5:23)

Being born again is a miracle. It is something that God must do for us because we cannot do it ourselves. It is also something that takes place spiritually. It is spiritual birth. It does not involve our physical body. We are born again spiritually, not physically. We were born the first time with a body, soul, and spirit (Hebrews 4:12; First Thessalonians 5:13). It is our spirit that must be born *again*. Our spirit is not born for the first time when we are saved. It is born *again*.

Being born again is a miracle. It is something that God must do for us because we cannot do it ourselves.

As I mentioned before, in Romans 7:22, Paul refers to his spirit, saying, "For I delight in the law of God after the inward man." The inward man refers to the spirit. This is in contrast to the outward body of flesh. Notice that the inward man delights in the Law of God. Paul's inward man was delighting in the Law of God because he was born again. He was not waiting to be born again. Being born again happens the moment you believe in Jesus Christ. There was nothing Paul had to do to earn the righteousness of his inward man. It was made righteous when he was born again. In the twinkling of an eye, at the moment he believed, God changed him, and his inward man was miraculously born again. This is a mountain moved.

You have a body, a soul, and a spirit. Your body is called the outward man. Your soul and spirit are called the inward man.

If you are following what Paul is saying, then you realize that when he was born again, his inward man was made different from his outward man. Prior to being born again, Paul's inward man and outward man were both sinful. Both were unrighteous in nature. Neither his body nor his spirit was righteous. He was a sinner inside and out. But when he was born again, his inward man was made righteous. Paul did not make his spirit righteous by doing anything to change it. God changed it. God miraculously made the unrighteous nature of Paul's spirit righteous.

When we are born again, our inward man is given God's righteousness. Romans 3:22 says, "Even the righteousness of God which is by faith of Jesus Christ unto all and upon all them that believe: for there is no difference." And Second Corinthians 5:17 says, "Therefore if any man be in Christ, he is a new creature: old things are passed away; behold, all things are become new."

The inward man of a Christian is born again with the righteousness of God. That makes the inward man new.

But the body of a Christian is still the same. It is unchanged. It still has the same sinful nature it was born with. This means that a Christian has two natures. Outwardly, the body has a sinful nature. Inwardly, the spirit has a righteous nature. This is the reason Paul says in Romans 7:17–21, "Now then it is no more I that do it, but sin that dwelleth in me. For I know that in me (that is, in my flesh,) dwelleth no good thing: for to will is present with me; but how to perform that which is good I find not. For the good that I would I do not: but the evil which I would not, that I do. Now if I do that I would not, it is no more I that do it, but sin that dwelleth in me. I find then a law, that, when I would do good, evil is present with me. For I delight in the law of God after the inward man."

> We are born again spiritually and made righteous inwardly, but the outward body stays the same.

Paul describes in this passage that his outward man sins and his inward man conforms to the Law of God. This is the experience of every Christian. We are born again spiritually and made righteous inwardly, but the outward body stays the same. The result is a war between doing right and wrong. We have the inward desire to do right and serve God, but the thoughts and impulses of the body still desire sin. Every Christian experiences a tug-o-war between the inward and outward self.

In Romans 4:22–24, Paul uses Abraham as an example of being made righteous, saying, "And therefore it was imputed to him for righteousness. Now it was not written for his sake alone, that it was imputed to him; But for us also, to whom it shall be imputed, if we believe on him that raised up Jesus our Lord from the dead." If you are a believer, you too have been born again and have been made righteous in the inward man. This is a miracle. Only God can make new birth happen. This is the reason salvation is only by the grace of God.

> *Believers are born again spiritually and are waiting for redemption of the body.*

I have taught this Biblical doctrine to many people, and invariably two questions are raised which are relevant to being a righteous man. First, if the inward man be made new with the righteousness of God, then is it possible for the righteous man to ever sin? Second, if the inward man cannot sin, then are we free to do as we please in the outward man and indulge in sins?

The answer to the first question is that the inward man is made with God's righteousness to prevent it from sinning. This is necessary to make salvation possible. God cannot stand to be in the presence of sin, and there is no sin in heaven. Speaking of God's intolerance of sin, Habakkuk 1:13 says, "Thou art of purer eyes than to behold evil, and canst not look on iniquity." God's aversion to sin explains why Revelation 21:27 says, "And there shall in no wise enter into it any thing that defileth, neither whatsoever worketh abomination, or maketh a lie: but they which are written in the Lamb's book of life."

The physical bodies of born-again believers are not changed at the time of salvation. When a Christian dies, his soul and spirit separate from his body. The body stays in the earth, dust to dust and ashes to ashes. It is sinful and not qualified to go to heaven. On the other hand, the soul and spirit (the inward man) are righteous and go to heaven without sin. At some point in the future, God will give every Christian a new body. Romans 8:23 says, "… even we ourselves groan within ourselves, waiting for the adoption, to wit, the redemption of our body." The body (the outward man) will be made sinless and righteous too. This is the only way to be qualified to enter heaven.

In the meantime, though the body is still sinful, the born-again inward man cannot sin, so it cannot die. Being born again, the inward man is miraculously made righteous by God. This prevents the inward man from sinning. Sin is not an option for the inward man. This guarantees the salvation of every Christian.

> *Effective prayers begin with the miracle of salvation.*

Romans 6:23 says, "For the wages of sin is death; but the gift of God is eternal life through Jesus Christ our Lord." Sin is the cause of death. Through new birth of the inward spirit, God secures the eternal future of every saved soul. Romans 6:22 says, "But now being made free from sin, and become servants to God, ye have your fruit unto holiness, and the end everlasting life." Life is everlasting because it cannot end. It cannot be terminated. It is forever. If it were temporary or conditional, then it would not be eternal.

Another interesting thing about eternal life comes from First John 5:12, which defines *life*, saying, "He that hath the Son hath life; and he that hath not the Son of God hath not life." The Biblical definition of *life* is all about having a relationship with the Son of God, Jesus Christ. Those who have a relationship with Christ are spiritually alive. They have spiritual life. Those who are separated from Jesus Christ are spiritually dead. So then, eternal life by Biblical definition is an eternal relationship with Jesus Christ. This relationship can never end because it is eternal. It is forever. This is how God ensures the miracle of eternal security.

This idea of being born again inwardly and being eternally secure raises the question in some minds, "If the inward man cannot sin, then are we free to do as we please in the outward man and indulge in sins?" After explaining the new birth in Christ, Paul dealt with this question in Romans 6:1, saying, "What shall we say then? Shall we continue in sin, that grace may abound?" And in Romans 6:15, he asks, "What then? shall we sin, because we are not under the law, but under grace?"

Paul gives two arguments for why a Christian should not indulge the sinful impulses of his outward man. First, he says being identified *in* Christ means that a Christian identifies *with* Christ. Just as Christ died to sin, we should consider ourselves dead to sin. Just as Christ is free of sin, we should think of ourselves as free from sin. Paul writes in Romans 6:11, "Likewise reckon ye also yourselves to be dead indeed unto sin, but alive unto God through Jesus Christ our Lord."

Second, he says a Christian should show *allegiance* to Christ, not to sin. As Christians, Christ has delivered us from being slaves to sin. Sin is no longer our master; therefore, we should not live as though we are slaves to sin. We should instead live for Christ. We called on Christ to save us because we wanted to escape sin and the consequences of sin. He delivered us, so we should look and behave like we are delivered.

These are the two reasons Paul gives to explain why Christians should not sin. As Christians, we should live like Christ because we *identify* with Christ, and we should live for Christ because we have *committed* ourselves to serve Him.

The Bible includes many exhortations to Christians to live for Christ because they struggle with temptations to sin. The outward man is always fighting to indulge in sins though the inward man always lives for God and refuses to sin.

Fortunately, the sins of the outward man cannot corrupt the

inward man. Therefore, the sins of the flesh cannot threaten the eternal life of the inward man. God secures eternal life for Christians by means of the new birth miracle which prevents the inward man from sinning. Because the inward man cannot sin, it cannot be condemned.

Paul explains how he is identified by his new inward man rather than by his old outward man, saying in Romans 7:17–18, "Now then it is no more I that do it, but sin that dwelleth in me. For I know that in me (that is, in my flesh,) dwelleth no good thing: for to will is present with me; but how to perform that which is good I find not." Paul is not excusing sin; he is explaining the ever-present battle he and every Christian have with the presence of sin in their bodies.

Many people wonder whether Christians will suffer any consequences for yielding to sin and for not controlling the carnal impulses of their bodies. The answer is yes. Paul says in First Corinthians 9:27, "But I keep under my body, and bring it into subjection: lest that by any means, when I have preached to others, I myself should be a castaway." It is possible to control the impulses of the body. Therefore, there is accountability to do so.

First Corinthians 3:11–15 explains the judgment of Christians, saying, "For other foundation can no man lay than that is laid, which is Jesus Christ. Now if any man build upon this foundation gold, silver, precious stones, wood, hay, stubble; Every man's work shall be made manifest: for the day shall declare it, because it shall be revealed by fire; and the fire shall try every man's work of what sort it is. If any man's work abide which he hath built thereupon, he shall receive a reward. If any man's work shall be burned, he shall suffer loss: but he himself shall be saved; yet so as by fire."

In this passage, Paul explains that the *foundation* of a Christian's life is built by and on Jesus Christ. This foundation makes the Christian's life permanently secure. What is built on the foundation is the life that we live. The righteous *works* of life are represented by gold, silver, and precious stones. The sinful *works* of life are represented by wood, hay, and stubble. Notice that the works of a Christian's life are built on the foundation of Christ. These works will be judged by fire. The works of sin will burn up, but the righteous works will last. And verse 15 states that, if our works burn up, we will suffer loss, but we are still saved. Why are we still saved if our works were sinful? Because the work of salvation, our foundation, is the work of Christ. The work of Christ cannot burn up, so the foundation of the Christian's life cannot burn up. Once we are saved, we are always saved by the mercy and grace of God.

The body (the outward man) that we are born with will never go to heaven. It is not born again. It still has a sin nature. Only the born-again inward man, which is the soul and spirit, will enter heaven. Salvation is secure because of the work of Christ. The Christian is judged for how he chooses to live, without risk of undoing the work of God.

Christians who choose to yield to sin are called *carnal* Christians. In First Corinthians 3:1, Paul rebukes carnal Christians in the church at Corinth, saying, "And I, brethren, could not speak unto you as unto spiritual, but as unto carnal, even as unto babes in Christ." The Corinthian Christians were saved but living in blatant sin, and so Paul was correcting them. As Paul explained in Romans 6, Christians should live like Christ and for Christ. Living right for Christ is sometimes called *sanctification*. It involves avoiding sin. Paul wrote in Second Timothy 2:21, "If a man therefore purge himself from these, he shall be a vessel unto honour, sanctified, and meet for the master's use, and prepared unto every good work."

Is it possible for Christians to choose a life of sin rather than to live for Christ? It is possible, but it would not make sense to do so. Becoming a Christian involves believing that God's way is the right way, desiring to be delivered from sin, and surrendering to live for Christ. It makes no sense to return to a life of sin when that is the very thing they desired to be delivered from. Such a decision would suggest that these people did not really repent with a genuine desire to be delivered from their sins.

Nonetheless, it is possible to be a carnal Christian. The church members in Corinth were carnal. Paul rebuked them, but he did not tell them they were not saved. Instead, he challenged them, saying in Second Corinthians 13:5, "Examine yourselves, whether ye be in the faith; prove your own selves. Know ye not your own selves, how that Jesus Christ is in you, except ye be reprobates?" His question addresses an important issue. If they were not living for Christ, *others* had reason to doubt that they were saved. If they were truly saved Christians, then they were carnal Christians. But if they were not truly saved, they were Christians in name only.

> *It is possible to think that you are a Christian and live like a Christian but not truly be a Christian.*

It may seem strange to you, but it is possible to think that you are a Christian and live like a Christian but not truly be a Christian. In Matthew 7:21–23, Jesus says, "Not every one that saith unto me, Lord, Lord, shall enter into the kingdom of heaven; but he that doeth the will of my Father which is in heaven. Many will say to me in that day, Lord, Lord, have we not prophesied in thy name? and in thy name have cast out devils? and in thy name done many wonderful works? And then will I profess unto them, I never knew you: depart from me, ye that work iniquity."

The first time I read this passage was in 1974, and I was disturbed by its implications. These people were not only living for Christ, they were casting out demons in Christ's name. And still God says He never knew them. Can you imagine the shock of thinking that you are a Christian and living like a Christian only to find out that you are not?

For those not born again and made righteous spiritually, the good works they have make no difference. Not being born again means that God did not change them and make them righteous. Therefore, regardless of their works, God will reject them. Salvation must be by the grace of God and by His work alone.

You can tell what their problem is by what they say to God. They are relying on their works to be accepted by God. But as I mentioned, good behavior and thoughts cannot make you acceptable in God's eyes. The only way to be accepted into heaven is to rely on God's mercy and grace. He must change what you are. Only His works can change your nature, making it righteous. Your works will never change what you are by nature.

God will change *anyone* willing to accept His work and His promise. No matter how bad someone has been, God is always willing to forgive. Why? Because in His eyes, every lost soul has the same sin nature and is undeserving of salvation, so every person must be changed regardless of their works.

Believers are righteous in the inward man because they are born again. They offer effective prayers because they are justified in God's eyes and are sanctified by the way they live. Their prayers avail much because they listen to the quiet voice of God.

Prayers that avail much require three essential criteria: faith, belief, and righteousness.

Understanding the importance of faith, belief, and righteousness caused me to realize why prayers of so many believers are denied. Believing that God will grant you what *you* want is not enough to move mountains. You must pray in righteousness, and you must believe in that which God reveals to you. If you are praying without faith, you have nothing from God to believe in or to pray for.

Prayers that avail much and that God grants encourage those who pray. But prayers that avail much require three essential criteria: faith, belief, and righteousness.

FOUR TYPES OF PRAYER

1) FOR PERSONAL DESIRE
2) FOR PERSONAL REVELATION
3) BECAUSE OF REVELATION
4) BECAUSE OF ANSWERS

Prayers of faith are offered with an understanding of how to pray and what to pray for. There are four types of prayers. With an understanding of how to distinguish these four types of prayers, you will know which types of prayers move mountains, and you will know what to expect of the other types. Adjusting your expectations with an understanding of how God answers will bless you and eliminate your frustrations.

Prayers *for what you want* sound like this: Please let me marry so and so; please give me *this* job; please make it possible for me to buy *this* house; please make it possible for me to get *this* car; please give the missionaries the financial support they need; please spare my life from this illness; please make this a good day for me. These are prayers *submitting* a request desired. These are the most common prayers. These are requests that express what you would like God to do. These are prayers of faith because you understand by faith that God can grant your request and that you have His permission to make your request. God wants us to make requests of Him. It reminds us that we are dependent on Him, and such prayers are part of our learning experience. We learn from the answers God gives.

Prayers *for revelation* (faith) sound like this: Lord, whom should I marry; what job should I take; where should I live; should I spend money on this; which missionaries should we support; should I pray for healing to live; should I buy this house; what is your will for my life at this time? These are prayers *asking* God to reveal His will. We are asking for specific knowledge that is not revealed in the Bible. The prayer of Abraham's servant is a good example of this type of prayer. He had no clue which girl to choose as a wife for Isaac, so he prayed and asked God to make it clear to him which girl would be God's choice. When God grants these prayers, then we can pray *because of revelation*.

Prayers *because of revelation* (faith) sound like Elijah's prayer when he said to God, "according to thy word have I done these things." They are prayers *confirming* what has been made known. When God reveals His will and you believe it and then pray for it in righteousness, it will happen. Nothing can prevent your prayer from being granted. Prayers *because of revelation* are always preceded by God revealing what He wants you to pray for. The prayer of salvation is an example of this type of prayer. When His promise is shared with you, He confirms it by faith. This means He reveals to you that He wants to save you. All you have to do is believe, and your prayer for salvation will be granted. This prayer is your belief in Him. It is the moment your relationship and conversation with Him begin.

Prayers *because of God's answer* sound like this: Thank you, Lord, for sending this person into my life. Thank you for the house that you gave us. Thank you for the finances you gave the missionaries last month to meet their needs. Thank you for the job I have. Thank you for giving me the best answer to my request. Prayers because of God's answer express *thankfulness* to God after receiving His answer. We would be excited if all of our prayers were granted because that would mean that every prayer request would have been pleasing to God.

To offer prayers that are granted every time would be thrilling! Is this possible? Yes. Psalm 37:4 says, "Delight thyself also in the LORD; and he shall give thee the desires of thine heart." I will explain later how to pray these kinds of prayers every time you pray.

As you learn more about each type of prayer, you will understand the type of prayer you are offering to God. You will adjust your expectations appropriately to the type of prayer that you offer, and you will experience satisfaction with every prayer.

Underlying these four types of prayers are *four foundational truths* revealed by God. 1) God is in control at all times. 2) God hears every prayer. 3) God answers every prayer. 4) God's answers are always the best answers. These four truths are understood by faith and in the Word of God. They serve as the basis for praying and expecting answers to every prayer.

MOUNTAINS AND MIRACLES

Looking at the big picture of prayer in my life, all four types of prayer had been a part of my experience. The prayer of salvation was my first and most important mountain-moving prayer, a *prayer because of revelation*. Then, as a growing Christian, I asked God to teach me about the prayers that move mountains. This was a *prayer of what I wanted*. When I learned that I had cancer, I prayed to understand what I should pray for. This was a *prayer for revelation*. After God revealed to me what I should pray for, then I was *praying because of revelation*. After I was declared to be free of cancer, I thanked the Lord. This was a *prayer because of God's answer*.

These were prayers of faith because I knew by faith that God wanted me to pray. I did not necessarily know what to pray for, but I did know by faith that I should pray. I knew by faith that He was always in control, that He hears every prayer, that He answers every prayer, and that every answer is the best answer. I was ready to offer mountain-moving prayers. Are you?

GREAT INSIGHTS TO REMEMBER

1. Prayers that move mountains require faith, belief, and righteousness.
2. Faith is not belief. Faith is what you believe in.
3. Faith is personalized revelation serving as proof from God to confirm truths that may not have physical verification.
4. Because revelation from God is the confirmation of His Word, God is ultimately the evidence for truth.
5. The Bible and faith are revelations from God. Both reveal God's Word, His truths, His promises, and His will.
6. Without a righteous nature, righteous behavior is not accepted by God.
7. God expects us to live every moment of our lives for Him, but He does not reveal every detail of what we should do every moment of our lives.
8. Prayers are effectual and fervent because they are offered by the righteous.
9. Prayers that move mountains often require that God reveal to us the mountain to be moved.
10. The first mountain to be moved in your life is the mountain of sin and condemnation. Believe God, and let Him move it.
11. Prayers for revelation are prayers asking God what to pray for.

12. Prayers for what you want are prayers of faith, knowing that God tells you to make your requests.

13. Prayers because of revelation are prayers because of knowing by faith what to pray for.

14. Prayers because of God's answer are prayers of thankfulness because God answered your prayer.

15. God is always in control. He hears every prayer. He answers every prayer. And every answer is the best answer.

4
MY MOUNTAIN

Trust in the LORD with all thine heart;
and lean not unto thine own understanding.
— Proverbs 3:5

I asked Dr. Hayward if he had ever successfully treated a patient with stage 4 Hodgkin's lymphoma. He said no.

I knew God had given me my mountain.

I had asked God to teach me about prayers that move mountains. I did not ask for cancer or a trial of any kind. I just wanted to know about prayers that move mountains. I was surprised when God answered my prayer with an actual mountain to move. I am glad now, but I was confused at the time.

GOD OR MEDICINE?

There was a day before penicillin was discovered when being infected with staph was a death sentence. Today, we can get an antibiotic shot and recover. It is easy to take for granted the achievements of medicine that have become so common to us. We wash our hands before surgery and before eating dinner. It helps to prevent sickness. We brush our teeth to prevent dental caries, abscesses, and fatal septicemia. Over time we have learned how to make living more comfortable and how to treat diseases like cancer. This is not failing to trust God. Using our brains, making discoveries, and using the knowledge from those discoveries is a way of thanking God for our intelligence and for the knowledge gained in His creation.

God has given us brains to use for our benefit. He has given us the ability to improve our lives and to invent technology and medicines. It is an insult to God not to use our brains and to live more intelligently today than yesterday.

Some ask if it is a lack of trust in God to use medicine to fight cancer and other diseases. They reason that if God heals, why resort to using medicine and doctors? But for a bone with a compound fracture or for a severed major artery, reasonable people would not refuse a doctor's help. Does this mean they lack trust in God?

Relying on God does not mean you should tempt Him by standing in front of a speeding truck, starving yourself, or refusing medical help. When Satan dared Jesus to jump off the pinnacle of the temple to let the angels catch Him before hitting the ground, Jesus said in Matthew 4:7, "… It is written again, Thou shalt not tempt the Lord thy God." Should you eat to stay alive? Why bother? Let God sustain you. If you do eat, why not eat poison and let God protect you? Obviously, there is no end to the ridiculous things we can imagine to tempt God with.

God designed humanity to be intelligent, not irrational. And with that intelligence we have learned how to treat many illnesses. Better treatments are being developed every day because of intelligently designed technology and medicines. When we use our God-given intelligence, we are blessed, and God is honored.

Relying on God does not mean you should tempt Him by standing in front of a speeding truck, starving yourself, or refusing medical help.

If the means to treat disease is available, God approves of it. Jesus referred to the beneficial purpose of doctors, saying in Luke 5:31, "They that are whole need not a physician; but they that are sick." Luke, one of Christ's faithful followers who was divinely inspired by God to write two of the New Testament books, was a physician. And Paul advised Timothy to drink a little wine for medicinal purposes to soothe his stomach ailment (First Timothy 5:23). Trusting God does not require that medicine and human inventions be shunned.

God designed humans to be intelligent. We have achieved many great things that honor God. But we have abused God's gift of intelligence to accomplish feats without God's approval. The tower of Babel, for example, was a monumental achievement without God's approval. It was the product of God-given, human ingenuity. Many inventions have been made by people who do not believe in God. And some have attempted to use their intelligence to disprove the existence of the God who created human intelligence. Regardless of how intelligence is used, all human intelligence and achievements are a testimony to the intelligent design of God's creation.

But trusting *only* in human ingenuity, technology, and skills is a mistake. If you have any experience in life, you already know that everyone makes mistakes. Everyone is flawed. The most intelligent people in the world are fallible, not to mention sinful, greedy, and selfish. So it is foolish to think that trusting *exclusively* in doctors is the best thing to do. Jeremiah 17:5 cautions, "Thus saith the LORD; Cursed be the man that trusteth in man, and maketh flesh his arm, and whose heart departeth from the LORD."

Second Chronicles 16:12 mentions King Asa as someone who relied exclusively on physicians and ignored God. "And Asa in the thirty and ninth year of his reign was diseased in his feet, until his disease was exceeding great: yet in his disease he sought not to the LORD, but to the physicians." The implication is that Asa would not have suffered as he did had he sought help from God. The lesson to learn here is that whether or not we seek help from doctors, we should always seek help from the Lord. Jeremiah 17:7 reassuringly says, "Blessed is the man that trusteth in the LORD, and whose hope the LORD is."

Those who advocate trusting God without the benefit of doctors and medicine to fight cancer have drawn an arbitrary line of what it means to trust God. Such advocates fail to demonstrate their trust in God by sitting in a field and waiting for God to send manna to feed them, to send them water to drink, and to shelter them from the weather. They "trust God" with the lives of other people and up to a point for themselves. But where do they draw the line between trusting and not trusting God? There is no answer because it is all arbitrary. And usually these people try to fit one shoe on all feet.

I am not questioning the sincerity of people who are trying their best to live well, reduce illness, and find healing. Although they are sincere, their facts and logic should still be examined.

My point is that drawing a line between trusting God and trusting medicine and science should be consistent. Those who draw arbitrary lines of right and wrong (sometimes with the use of Scripture) should be challenged to be consistent when they draw their lines if they expect others to live by those lines too. When it comes to claims of relying on prayer without doctors and medicine, they should be challenged, for example, about where those lines are drawn when they break a bone in their arm. Can they trust God when they ask a doctor to set their bones? If so, then they should be able to trust God when they get a shot of penicillin or receive medicine for fighting cancer.

When the Bible and God are brought into the discussion about when to use medicine and doctors, I like to refer to Romans 14:5, which says, "One man esteemeth one day above another: another esteemeth every day alike. Let every man be fully persuaded in his own mind." This verse is talking about how to live for God, not about choosing to sin. It is talking about rules people *invent* to live for God. Sadly, God gets blamed for a lot of decisions He has nothing to do with.

> Sadly, God gets blamed for a lot of decisions He has nothing to do with.

The commands God expects us to live by are those He writes about in His Word. Nonetheless, if someone feels convinced that doing something is sin, for which there is no Scriptural guidance, they should not do it. God may be revealing a restriction for one person and not for others. This could be a faith-based decision, rather than Scripture-based. The lesson in Romans 14 is that if you think God wants you to do something, obey Him. If it is not written down for everyone to obey, then keep it to yourself.

Of course, God will never contradict His Word, so anything known by faith will not violate God's written instructions. But it is the tendency of people to invent new rules to apply God's instructions. These are typically justified as clarifications and extensions of God's Word to ensure correct obedience. It is often done sincerely, though sincerely wrong.

> *Why should God's people stay ignorant because someone else decides to misuse knowledge for evil rather than for good?*

Paul says to keep the shoe of faith on your own foot. If one man eats meat to the glory of God, then let him do so. And if another refuses to eat meat to the glory of God, then let him do so (Romans 14:3–6). Both have made choices to glorify God; and God's Word does not warn either about doing as they desire in this case. Like I said, this is not about choosing to sin and violate the Word of God.

I am not afraid of medical technology and the exploration of creation. I am fascinated by it and awed by the incredible design built into creation. I think God wants us to learn as much as we can about His creation and to use that knowledge. Sure, it is possible to use knowledge for evil. But the fact that some abuse knowledge is no reason for the rest of us to shun knowledge. It is irrational to allow the choices of others to dictate our choices. Why should God's people stay ignorant because someone else decides to misuse knowledge for evil rather than for good? Believers should be at the forefront of scientific exploration, discovering more about God's creation, its amazing design, how to care for it, and how to use it.

TREATMENT PLAN

In the world of medicine, new discoveries are made every day, so I searched articles to find out if new treatments had been found for Hodgkin's lymphoma. I took an article I found to Dr. Hayward to discuss the option of using a new chemotherapy at the time abbreviated as ABVD.

As I mentioned earlier, I was reading as much as I could about Hodgkin's lymphoma and what was being used to treat it. MOPP was the treatment of choice at the time, but the side effects were very unpleasant. Dr. Hayward had not treated patients with the ABVD regimen yet, but he was willing to try it for three months. If it seemed to produce positive results, then we would continue to use it to the completion of the chemo session.

PREPARING FOR CHEMOTHERAPY

Knowing Dr. Hayward was willing to try the experimental ABVD chemo drugs was a great relief to me because I dreaded the effects of the chemo treatments using MOPP. As I mentioned before, I had visited a man in a nearby town who had been treated for Hodgkin's lymphoma ten years earlier. The story he had to tell was disturbing. He told me about the numerous tests they did on him, the painful experience of the lymphangiogram, the laparotomy (stage 3 surgery), the removal of his spleen, and the bone marrow biopsy without anesthesia.

The MOPP protocol had debilitated his body so that, even ten years after the treatment, he did not have the energy to hold down his regular job as a floor tile contractor. His wife told me that every day when she came home from work she found him in bed sleeping.

He said that after a chemo treatment, he had about one hour to get home before the vomiting started. The nausea and vomiting lasted for two days. His treatments were extended an additional two months due to delays caused by low blood cell counts. The experience was so traumatic that he finished his treatments only because his wife and friends dragged him to the doctor's office. After talking to him about MOPP, I was ready to avoid it before I even started. I shared this with Dr. Hayward, but he reassuringly told me there were new drugs to help relieve the nausea and vomiting. In my case, Ativan and Compazine were used to make me feel more comfortable.

A typical chemo session involved having an IV line connected to the port-a-cath in my chest, being sedated, and then dripping the chemo drugs into my blood. Afterwards, Colleen or friends that were with me for the treatments walked me out to the car and drove me home and put me to bed. I was sleepwalking, so I do not remember any of it. Colleen gave me Benadryl to sustain my sleep, but within half an hour after taking that pill, I was vomiting. I do remember that part. However, once this was over, I went back to sleep and did not wake up until the next day.

One of the best things I did was ask for a port-a-cath. I learned about this device from my cousin who is a cardiologist. The chemo drugs given to me are caustic to the blood vessels, and sometimes phlebitis, which is inflammation of the blood vessels, can develop. Without a port-a-cath, blood vessels can become unusable, so other arteries have to be used. The port-a-cath is used to deliver the drugs into the big vein leading directly to the heart. This route dilutes the drugs into a bigger volume of blood, and sometimes the drugs can be delivered more quickly this way. I chose an internal port-a-cath, which is sewn under the skin of your chest. It was wonderful because it was barely visible, and being under the skin, it was protected from external contamination.

Treatments were every other week. For the first week after chemo, I was usually nauseous and in declining health. The second week, my body was recovering and getting stronger, which allowed me to take another treatment. On two occasions, the doctor postponed treatments because I needed an extra week to build up more strength and blood cells.

In preparation for the chemo treatments, I bought some cans of liquid food supplements. But I had a hard time drinking them because of the taste and texture. I did not cut my hair, which was short anyway. As it turned out, only half of my hair fell out, and it fell out evenly. It made me wonder if people who had cut their hair had done so unnecessarily.

Another very helpful thing I did was to take mint gum with me to the doctor's office. I did not chew it, but sniffing the mint during the procedure helped reduce the feeling of nausea. After several treatments, even the smell of alcohol and betadine made me feel sick, so the mint came in handy.

WHEN THE CURE IS WORSE THAN THE DISEASE

My grandmother died of cancer around 1980, and at that time, it was said that most people were dying of the treatment rather than the disease. I was dreading the effects of chemo.

As I mentioned earlier, the new chemotherapy regimen for Hodgkin's lymphoma at the time was called ABVD, which is an abbreviation for the combination of drugs Adriamycin ® (doxorubicin), Bleomycin, Vinblastine, and Dacarbazine (DTIC). The side effects were less severe with ABVD than with MOPP. It did not have the track record of MOPP at the time, but it appeared promising with early success rates similar to that of MOPP. It was a welcomed alternative.

Not knowing what to expect, I thought about quality of life. Why choose the prolonged misery of chemotherapy rather than the comfort of a shorter life? But I could not shake the idea that God wanted me to trust Him for recovery. It was impossible for me to consider any other option than pursuing the chemo treatment. God would take care of me, even if that meant death by chemo.

Unlike chemotherapy, God's cure for sin is always an improvement. Being born again gives you a new spirit with new desires to live for God and a new disposition to retrain your physical body to think right and do right. The retraining is not always easy, but it makes life better. To be able to walk in peace with God rather than in anger, bitterness, and fear, which so many people struggle with, is much better.

Regardless of the hardships in life, First Corinthians 10:13 promises, "There hath no temptation taken you but such as is common to man: but God [is] faithful, who will not suffer you to be tempted above that ye are able; but will with the temptation also make a way to escape, that ye may be able to bear [it]." Anyone can be content in Christ when they are confident in Him. And the greater the hardship in life, the more amazing your testimony is if contentment is evident in your life.

What state of mind are you in? Are you content? Are you able to turn your hardships into opportunities? Everyone shares in hardships that come with this life. Some suffer more than others. But if we are content, the hardships do not define who we are. The contentment does.

> *If we are content, the hardships do not define who we are. The contentment does.*

CHOOSING REMEDIES FOR LONG-TERM BENEFIT

Cancer treatment has come a long way in thirty years. There are some promising treatments being tested today that will reduce side effects and hopefully eliminate the killing of healthy cells while killing cancer cells.

At the time of my chemotherapy treatments, there were over 200 drugs being used to treat different cancers. My treatments were harsh. I felt like my body was a toxic waste dump. I was putting into my body drugs that healthy people would never want to be exposed to for fear of ruining their health.

But this was the best remedy available for my kind of cancer. I know there are alternative medicine claims that sound very appealing. It is understandable that people will seek alternatives because they promise fewer side effects. Many claim remedies that will improve the body's immune system so it can heal itself. Anything that will strengthen the immune system and improve health is good. But many claims are exaggerated. Some are outright dishonest.

A friend of mine chose a diet plan for bladder cancer. Three months later the tumors were gone. It was an amazing testimony of how his diet brought about healing. His testimony was included in a book as a success story. A year later, he died. The tumors in the bladder were gone, but the cancer had spread to other organs in his body. His diet was apparently useful only on the tumors in the bladder, not elsewhere. His death did not make it into the book.

Medicine is based on research and statistics. Sure-fire cures for cancer have not been discovered. Doctors recommend what is known to work best at the time with the best odds for success.

The fact is most of the best remedies for cancer are still painful. Some treatments are more dreadful than others, but without them, cancer would take your life. Each person must talk to his or her doctor, learn about available treatments, and make a prayerful, informed decision. Most people who choose to suffer through the treatment will live longer than those who choose to do nothing.

Life is full of tough choices that sometimes involve suffering in the short run for long-term benefits. My younger daughter, who was six years old at the time, one day was complaining about a sore on the back of her leg. It looked like an infected brown recluse spider bite to me. It was swollen, darkened, a red soft crater in the middle, infected, and painful. I took her to the emergency room at the hospital, and the doctor had the same opinion, that it was a brown recluse bite. He said he would have to lance it and get the pus out. But he would have to do it without anesthesia. Anesthesia could delay wound healing and complicate the infection. I held her hand tight as she screamed because of the pain. The procedure was successful, and the wound healed. But in order to heal, my daughter suffered excruciating pain. Her preference would have been to avoid the pain. But the infection would have worsened and eventually would have killed her. Sometimes enduring pain is necessary to gain long-term benefits.

Spiritually, it is difficult to admit and confess guilt for being sinful, but it must be done to enjoy the long-term blessings of eternal life. The alternative is eternal death.

Christ endured unimaginable suffering to pay for our sins. If there had been another way, He would have done it. The fact that Jesus died for us is evidence that there was no other way. He dreaded His death and the suffering He was going to endure. He even prayed to His Father, "If possible let this cup pass me by." But after saying this, He added, "Nevertheless, not my will but thine be done." Jesus did not look forward to enduring the torment of eternal condemnation. He willingly suffered because of His eternal love for us and our eternal need. Because of His willingness to suffer for us, salvation and eternal life are possible.

PREPARING FOR DEATH

> Death is inevitable, so preparing for death is common sense.

If you are battling cancer, do not quit. Never quit. Don't be robbed of days you could share with loved ones. If you win your battle, you may have many years to go. But you will never know unless you keep fighting for your life.

Nonetheless, death is inevitable. Everyone dies. This is stating the obvious. But isn't it strange how death is ignored and treated as if it will never happen? If you accept the fact that you will inevitably die, and perhaps sooner than you expect, you know you should prepare for death. Because death can come unexpectedly, it is important to prepare for eternity now rather than later. Second Corinthians 6:2 says, "… behold, now is the accepted time; behold, now is the day of salvation."

Once you are saved, you can look death in the face and not be afraid. Why? Because though your physical body will die, your soul will not. When you die physically, you just transition from life on Earth to life in heaven. This does not mean you do not feel the emotions of anxiety and dread of dying. Death is something people would prefer to avoid. But for believers, physical death is simply the beginning of a better life in heaven.

If you have time to prepare for death, begin by reviewing and adjusting your goals and priorities. Live life to its fullest. Make the most of your time now while you are alive. Don't worry about dying. Just prepare for it, and live now to do something meaningful with your life.

When I realized I could die sooner than I expected, my goals changed because my timeline and priorities changed. My prayers intensified and were more frequent. I spent more time meditating on God's Word. The things that no one else could do became my priorities. I could not put them off any more.

My health was a priority, and so my schedule had to be adjusted. I spent more time with my family, and I prioritized doing what I could to make the transition to being without me easier for my family. Getting my house in order was important for those I would leave behind. My death would affect more than just me.

CONCERN FOR THOSE LEFT BEHIND

If you have lost someone close to you and have been involved in making decisions about the funeral, finances, and children, then you know the stress of figuring out what to do after someone dies.

You can reduce the stress your loved ones will experience when you die by doing just a few simple things. This will take you minutes but could save those left behind hours and even weeks of time.

Being concerned for those you leave behind is natural, especially if you have small children or other dependent family members. Ironically, while people were concerned for me, I was more concerned about them. If my life were shortened, I would not have to worry about planning for the future like they would.

The health crisis I faced did not affect just me. It affected my family. My biggest concern was making the possible transition from being married to being widowed easier for Colleen. God was in control, so I did not have to be concerned about what He would do. The concern was if I were doing all that I could do.

Would Colleen be a widow with a child to raise? Would she be able to work part-time? Would we be able to reduce the overhead of living before I died?

I was praying and asking God for healing, but I felt responsible to do what I could to help Colleen and Lisa. Colleen's boss was very helpful and let her do some work from home. She had already been working from home while on maternity leave. She had been preparing to quit her job to stay at home and raise Lisa. But when we discovered I had cancer, those plans changed. Through her, we had additional income, and we had insurance. If she had quit, we would have been without insurance.

If we could reduce the overhead by paying off our mortgage, then she could work part-time and take care of Lisa. We always lived debt free, so the house was the only debt we had. Since there was no penalty to pay the mortgage off early, we decided to pay it off quickly. We added a little extra above the regular mortgage payment. We also paid the monthly amount with two payments every two weeks rather than once a month, which resulted in the equivalent of one month's additional payment at the end of the year. And because the savings account we had was earning less than our mortgage rate, we put our monthly savings toward the mortgage. We knocked years off of our payments, and the house was paid for in five years. Being completely debt free meant that Colleen would be able to work part-time and take care of Lisa without worrying about a mortgage and debt.

I did not have to worry about my ministry responsibilities. I have always worked with the objective of training others to replace me. At the time, the campus ministry and discipleship ministries were in good hands. And if God were intending to take me out of this life, I knew He had replacements prepared. I had no doubt that God had everything under control.

FINAL INSTRUCTIONS

One thing you can do to help those you leave behind is to write a note of final instructions. These instructions are for whoever ends up with the responsibility of settling your accounts of assets and liabilities. It can be a long list or simply the name of your lawyer or your bank. Even if you do not have a family, you will want to decide what to do with your estate. You can help your church and missionaries. At the very least, you should have friends that you would like to give to.

The note of final instructions tells where to find your last will and testament, your trust, insurance policies, bank account, and subscriptions. Make sure the final instructions can be found by someone you trust. These instructions should include personal information including your social security number, which is needed to access bank accounts, make insurance claims, and file one last income tax report.

Here is a list of documents to prepare. You may not want to prepare all of these, but I list them as recommendations.

1. Final Instructions with personal data and accounts (keep the original in a safety box)
2. Trust Agreement
3. Trust Abstract
4. Pour-over Will
5. Advance Directive
6. Durable Power of Attorney (POA)
7. Living Will
8. Healthcare POA
9. Conservator for probate court: spouse, family member, friend, pastor
10. Healthcare Proxy

A LIVING TRUST OR A LAST WILL AND TESTAMENT

I was listening to a radio program one day and heard a man talking about living trusts. I was intrigued because he said a trust was the best way to distribute your assets and to protect your underaged children if you were to die. A trust allows you to avoid probate court and lawyer fees. It leaves a trusted family member, or friend, or institution of your choice in control to carry out your instructions. And you can assign more than one person to carry out different instructions. Other benefits of a trust include reducing your estate and gift taxes; avoiding the delay, publicity, and expense of probate court; and protecting your estate from creditors and lawsuits.

On the other hand, if you use a last will and testament, or if you leave no instructions at all, your estate will automatically go into probate court. A court-appointed judge will decide what will happen to your possessions and children. There will be court fees and lawyer fees, and the process could take months.

I decided to use a trust for our estate. I bought a book about living trusts, read it, and answered a list of questions to prepare my own trust. Then I hired an estate lawyer, discussed my goals, answered more questions, and let him draft the finalized trust.

Our daughter was our biggest concern. Our decision about what would happen to her if both Colleen and I were no longer around was the most important instruction to include in our trust, both in the way of caregivers and finances.

The lawyer that Colleen and I talked to was a kind, elderly man. He told us that he was a big advocate of using trusts rather than a last will and testament. His personal experience with probate court after his mother's death was fraught with delays and problems that could have been avoided with a trust. He also said that he believed that no estate was too small to put in a trust.

Prepare your trust while your estate is small. A simple trust is less expensive, and you can change it as your family and estate change. For those left behind and grieving, having a trust is much easier than not having one.

Determine what you can do to be helpful, but don't try to rule from the grave. Some people try to control the future even after their death by leaving all kinds of instructions. The problem is that no one knows the changes in circumstances that might arise. When you die, it is time to let go and let someone else make decisions. The time to help others make good choices is while you are alive, not after you are dead. Fortunately, God is in control, and He has been helping generation after generation make the transition after the deaths of loved ones. Your death will be no different.

LIVING WILL

One of the deacons in my church passed away years ago due to an unusual accident. While setting up a display in a store, he fell off the ladder and hit his head. He went into a coma. In the hospital, decisions had to be made about how to treat him and, in the end, whether to take him off life support.

I felt very sorry for his wife. She found herself in the middle of a tug-o-war between family and friends, some advising her to stop life support and others wanting her to continue. Both sides considered the decision a moral issue. Regardless of the decision she made, she would be condemned for making the wrong choice. The stress and frustration created by these two camps was the last thing she needed to deal with while grieving over the prospect of losing her husband. Had he prepared an advance directive, also known as a living will, his wife could have been spared the additional emotional stress during this crisis.

The living will goes by different names in different states and countries. It documents your instructions to help others make medical decisions for you if you are not able to. If you have a living will, the doctors and family members will know your wishes and won't have to guess what you would want. A simple living will and a designated loved one you trust to act on your behalf with the power of attorney will ensure that your wishes are carried out. This may reduce emotional duress and could be a gift of love for those you leave behind.

SAYING GOODBYE

For most people, having the opportunity to say goodbye is important. If you were to die suddenly or become incapacitated and could not communicate, what would you like loved ones to know? It would be nice to have a letter that could be found someday if you were to die without an opportunity to express your love and appreciation. You can write your thoughts now and then edit your letter up until the time you die.

Here are five things to consider putting into your letter or video to family and friends.

1. Say thank you generally and specifically. Mention specific moments if possible.
2. Apologize.
3. Forgive.
4. Express your love.
5. End with an encouraging thought about why you are prepared to see Jesus in heaven and that you will be waiting to see them again.

PREPARING FOR YOUR FUNERAL

Funerals are for the living. The dead are gone and enjoying a new life if they resolved their differences with God before dying. Those left behind will make decisions for the funeral. But your input will be a big help. My experience in helping families with funerals is that families want to honor the deceased, so they are concerned with what the deceased would have liked.

Leaving instructions and information for your trustee or loved ones concerning your funeral would be helpful. If possible, make arrangements to pay for your funeral with insurance or savings. Grieving over a death is a lot of stress, so if you have already thought about which funeral home to contact and have already prepaid for the burial plot and funeral, that would take a lot of stress off of those left behind.

Select a funeral home, and give them instructions to keep in your file to make available to your loved ones. You will also want to keep a set of instructions in your safe deposit box.

Here are seven things to consider recommending for your funeral.

1. Which funeral home?
2. What kind of funeral service?
3. Where to hold the funeral service?
4. Burial or cremation?
5. Music?
6. What clothes would you like to be buried in?
7. Have you prepared a written goodbye to be read during the funeral?

Some might question whether preparing for my death showed a lack of faith. It did not. It was the right thing to do; and through prayer, God reassured me strongly that it was the right thing to do.

The steps Colleen and I took were very beneficial to us. I would not have paid off my house, written out a trust, or prepared a living will without facing a life-and-death crisis. But because these decisions were made, we were wiser for the experience and better prepared for an unexpected death, not only mine, but Colleen's too. We did what most people wait too long to do and wish they had done sooner. We now encourage others to learn from our personal experience.

WHAT LIFE IS LIKE DURING CHEMO

It was helpful to have family members stay with us at the beginning of my chemo treatments as we were learning what to expect. Colleen's mother and my parents were able to come from California a few times to help us. Also, it was helpful to have them at the house at the end of the chemo treatments when I was not able to get around well.

My first treatment was on a Monday. I went to Dr. Hayward's office and sat in the comfortable, overstuffed, reclining chair. His nurse, Carol, administered the chemo treatment. Anti-nausea drugs were not used in 1989 to reduce the nausea and vomiting, so patients were put to sleep with a sedative. Ativan and Compazine were used to put me to sleep. As I felt the sedatives taking effect, I told Colleen I would see her tomorrow. One side effect of the sedatives was that, for about five minutes before I fell asleep, my legs became very fidgety, and I could not get comfortable. It made me want to climb the walls. I did not discover until after the treatments were over that the Compazine was the cause of my agitation.

After a treatment when leaving the doctor's office out the back door, whoever had come to help me during the treatment walked me to the car. Getting from the car into the house was more of a challenge because I had two steps and a threshold to walk up.

About an hour after arriving home, Colleen would wake me up to give me Benadryl. I do not remember many of the occasions of being awakened by Colleen, but I do remember waking up once or twice in the first twenty-four hours after being treated to run to the bathroom and vomit. But then I would go right back to sleep. Personally, I found it better to prepare for the nausea and vomiting by not eating the night before being treated.

The first treatment was different from the others. After being awakened for the Benadryl, I stayed awake and asked for a peanut butter sandwich. Colleen told me to go back to sleep because I should not be awake. But I was hungry. As I recall, I did get my sandwich, but only Colleen knows for sure. After the other treatments, I was not asking for anything to eat or drink until I woke up the next day.

Chemotherapy is hard on the body. The chemicals are chosen

because of their killing effect on cancer cells. The theory is that the faster a cell grows, the faster it will be killed by the chemo drugs. But cancer cells are not the only cells in your body that grow fast. This is the reason that your hair stops growing and falls out; your digestive system shuts down, resulting in constipation or diarrhea; your bone marrow cells are suppressed, slowing the production of blood cells; and sores might develop in your mouth. These cells are fast-growing cells in your body. However, all cells in your body are being attacked. Treatments are scheduled to allow your body time to recover enough to be dosed with the chemo drugs again. The trick is to kill the cancer cells before killing you.

People are affected differently by chemo drugs. As I mentioned before, there are over 200 chemicals used to treat people. And people of different ages and health react differently. Also, different cancers react differently to the chemicals.

Perhaps the most commonly discussed side effect of chemotherapy is hair loss (alopecia). The nurses in Dr. Hayward's office were taking bets on how long it would take before I lost my hair. It usually takes two weeks for most people to notice hair loss. Some lose their hair near the end of their treatment, and some do not lose much hair. On the other hand, some talk about their hair changing texture and color. For me, my beard stopped growing twenty-one days after treatments began. It was week five when I noticed my pillow was full of hair one morning. When it fell out, it happened overnight. I did not lose all of it. But there was a lot on the pillow. My hair stopped growing and continued to fall out over time. I might have lost half of my hair in total, so it didn't seem too bad to me. I did notice that all the gray hairs fell out. And every time I took a shower, I had to unclog the drain.

One man told me about using a particular brand of shampoo for thinning, frail hair to reduce the loss of hair. I used it. Could it be that half of my hair did not fall out because of using that shampoo? Perhaps it was my high calorie, high protein diet.

Perhaps it was my age. Perhaps my hair grows slowly. Perhaps it was a combination of factors. We will never know.

One interesting characteristic during chemo was that injuries didn't heal normally. While changing the tire on my car, I lost my grip on the tire iron, and it scratched my forearm. It was a minor scratch, but I still washed it and rubbed an antibiotic cream on it to prevent infection. Though it was just a minor scratch, it healed abnormally. I actually have a scar as a result of the cells failing to repair the skin properly. Under normal circumstances, I would not have thought twice about it, and it would have healed without evidence of injury. The fast-growing repair cells did not heal normally. If a minor scratch leaves scar tissue, then think what a major injury during chemotherapy would do.

Constipation is another predictable and troubling side-effect. The digestive tract shuts down, and I think this contributed to some of the nausea I experienced. A liquid diet of protein drinks, juice, and soups was beneficial for the first week after chemo treatment. Some people talk about not eating, but I was hungry, so eating was not a problem for me. In fact, I gained twenty pounds in my six months of chemo. I did not feel good, but I was hungry. Eating made me feel a little better and helped me gain weight.

Gaining weight was unexpected. I was not supposed to gain weight based on the experiences of others. But I did. I'd never been overweight, so this was a new experience for me. I remember being at the doctor's office and reaching over the coffee table in the waiting room to get a magazine. I did not feel stiff, but there was resistance to leaning forward. Then all of a sudden, a shelf of skin and fat shot out of my stomach. My skin did not know how to fold fat, so it all just formed a single shelf. I laughed out loud when I realized what happened because it was so odd.

Choosing what you eat will help you manage eating and

digestive problems. As I already mentioned, nausea was a problem I had with chemotherapy. I was nauseous because my body was reacting to the drugs, and I was nauseous because my digestive system shut down for about six days after each treatment. I was on a liquid diet for the first week after being treated. The second week, I ate whatever I wanted. I was usually hungry, so my appetite was back to normal during the second week. I also rotated my diet plan with different foods to avoid associating particular foods with nausea. I am prone to do that. Rotating through a variety of foods did help. I only had problems with a couple of foods after several treatments. But my aversion to them did not last more than a couple of years.

For six days after being treated, typically I declined in health. As the drugs were attacking the cancer cells, they were attacking my healthy cells at the same time. But the effects were not enough to prevent me from participating in meetings, teaching Bible studies, counseling, discipling, leading the college ministry, serving as the associate pastor, overseeing the discipleship ministry, and helping my wife raise our baby girl. I was in bed for two days every other week and nauseous a few times a month, but for the most part, I was active. And by the second week of each treatment, I was walking around feeling somewhat normal. I was able to mow the lawn, work on the car, and do other physically demanding work. As the treatments progressed every other week, I was weakening, so I spent more time writing and teaching about prayer.

CARING FOR YOURSELF

The following recommendations will help you avoid difficulties during chemotherapy.

Doctor–patient roles

1. It is important for you to be involved in caring for yourself.

The doctor will help you diagnose problems and recommend treatments. But you must take responsibility for your own health. Learn as much as you can. Prepare questions to ask the doctor. Ask about options that he might have to offer or that you have read about. My treatment with ABVD was due to finding an article describing its success. I talked with the doctor about using that regimen of drugs instead of MOPP.

2. It is up to you to choose between options your doctor gives you. It is up to you to follow the doctor's instructions. It is up to you to care for yourself at home. It is up to you to eat right, sleep well, and exercise. It is up to you to describe your symptoms to the doctor and tell him when and how these symptoms appeared. The more information you give the doctor, the better his diagnosis and treatment recommendations will be.

3. Keep your own health chart. The doctor has expertise, but you are responsible for your health, for giving him information about your health and symptoms, and for following his instructions. I used a daily calendar to keep track of my symptoms. I could have done more such as record my heart rate and describe the color of my skin, the redness of my eyelids, my diet, the frequency of going to the bathroom, my sleep schedule, my temperature, and more. I confess I lacked the motivation to keep a record of more details than I did. It would have helped to print out a blank record sheet of details to keep track of each day. But instead, I wrote down symptoms on the calendar when something very unusual occurred like chills and a temperature spike.

4. Consider using a printed chart to write a summary report for your primary care physician. This will help the doctor focus on the most relevant and current information about

your health. I write a very brief time chart summary of my past health conditions and a report of symptoms I am concerned about. I even include a graph to show the change and trend in numbers reported on my tests. The better the information is understood, the better the diagnosis and treatment.

5. Taking care of yourself requires that you learn about your disease and what other patients have done. I am writing this book to help you and others take care of yourselves physically and spiritually. You are reading and being informed. It is up to you to learn more about your health and disease. The fact is informed patients live longer.

6. It is important to ask your doctor and your pharmacist about foods that you should avoid. Some chemo drugs do not mix well with certain foods. Some patients consult with a nutritionist for their diet plan.

7. It is important to keep track of your temperature because a rising temperature could indicate an infection. For chemo patients, this is a serious warning. The doctor needs to examine you right away to make sure you do not have an infection. An infection will make you feel worse and possibly put you in a life threatening predicament.

Hygiene

1. Your skin is your first line of defense against infection. A scratch in your skin is a breach in defense and an opportunity for infection. This could be a disaster for someone whose health and immune system are weakened by the chemo treatment. Keep your skin clean with normal bathing and hygiene habits. Wash and put medicine on injuries, cuts, and scrapes. These are potential infection points on your body.

2. Brush your teeth and gums carefully so you do not scrape

your mouth. For some patients on chemo, mouth sores occur. Mine were not frequent, but when they appeared, they were very painful. Sometimes stomach ulcers can also occur. The doctor can give you medicine to treat these sores.

3. Use your own toothbrush and your own towel in the bathroom.
4. Keep your feet clean and dry to avoid fungus infections. You will feel warmer and more comfortable.
5. Blow your nose carefully. If your sinuses are becoming congested, you will develop an infection. The goal is to keep your sinuses clear and draining to avoid trapping bacteria in your sinuses. This can happen because of allergies or a virus. Either way, talk to your doctor about a recommended decongestant that you can use. If you blow your nose with too much pressure, the mucus will be pushed into your inner ear tube. That will lead to an inner ear infection and complicate your health condition. This problem is easy to avoid by blowing your nose gently and using a decongestant.

Precautions

1. Depending on the weakness of your immune system, be careful when in crowds, especially during sickness seasons. If possible, avoid direct contact like shaking hands. Keep hands away from your face, mouth, and nose. And wash your hands after shaking hands or touching things in public like handrails on stairs, escalators, etc.
2. Be alert to people coughing and sneezing, and avoid them.
3. You are what you eat, and you eat what you buy. Your body needs nourishment to repair itself. It needs all the help it can get while going through chemotherapy. So it is important that you supply your body with nutrients vital for its repair and defense.

4. Prepare menus, recipes, and a grocery list.

5. Clean and cook your food very well. Your digestive tract is not functioning normally, and if you have a weak immune system, your gut is not able to protect you as well. It is important to avoid contaminating yourself by ingesting harmful germs from dirty foods.

6. Apple juice, prune juice, and carrot juice are good for constipation once your bowels begin to move again. Bananas and cheese are good for controlling diarrhea.

7. If you are taking pills or powders at home for your chemo treatment, be very careful about exposing your family members to these drugs. Chemo agents are carcinogenic and will do them harm. I know this sounds strange because these drugs are going into your body. But like I said earlier, the best methods we know of at this time to treat cancer are drugs that kill cancer cells before they kill you. There are some exciting treatments being tested that do no harm, but they are not available yet.

8. Minimize your exposure to direct sunlight and protect yourself from sunburn.

Other things to do

1. Drink plenty of water to keep your body hydrated and to help reduce damage to your kidneys. Most drugs will flush out of your body within forty-eight hours, but some can last up to seven days.

2. Reduce stress, and get plenty of rest to let your body heal after each chemo treatment.

3. Take time to meditate on priorities and goals. Be thoughtful about your life and how to be helpful to others.

4. Make a reminder list of things to do.

5. Keep your mind active by praying, reading books, listening to podcasts, doing puzzles, setting goals, talking to friends, reaching out to others to encourage them, taking a walk if possible, and working on projects.

RECOVERY FROM CHEMOTHERAPY

In October 1989, eight months after beginning chemo, I completed my last treatment. The blood tests and CT scan showed no signs of cancer in my body. If there were residual cancer cells left, it would be important for my body to be able to kill those cells. So a quick recovery of my health and strengthening of my immune system were important. My body was in need of repair.

The drugs used for my chemotherapy were caustic, and I knew the drugs had damaged my body, but to what extent? The liver enzymes were elevated, which indicated damage to the liver. My short-term memory was diminished at least by half of what it had been. The CT scan suggested there was scarring in my bone marrow. I do not know what damage was done to other organs, but there were no indications that signaled an alarm. My heart and kidneys were still working.

Follow-up care is important after treatment. Regular doctor appointments were set for every six months for three years. After that, doctor visits were once a year. These appointments included CT scans to monitor lymph node sizes and blood tests. I also kept a journal of changes in health.

It has been reported that Hodgkin's lymphoma survivors who live beyond five to ten years are at higher risk of developing serious side-effects from their chemo treatments. The immune systems of Hodgkin's lymphoma patients tend to be weakened, so fighting cancer and disease is diminished. For example, leukemia is much more likely to occur.

Because my body was weakened, it was important to do things to recover my health. My cardiovascular recovery was my first concern, so I began swimming every day until I was swimming 1,000 meters daily. In high school, this was a warm up before swim training began for the day, but during my recovery it was a sufficient workout. My strength and agility were returning quickly.

My diet was nothing special. I just made sure that I was eating what would be called a good balance of proteins and carbohydrates from meats, fruits, vegetables, and grains.

POST RECOVERY

I recovered quickly, and in a short time, every day was filled once again with work and responsibilities in ministry, business, and family again. I even began a new project producing television programs for our ministry through the Community Access Television station.

As I said before, your body fights off cancer cells throughout your life, maybe even daily. Most people have healthy immune systems that are able to fight off cancer and disease. But once cancer overwhelms your immune system, you are at a higher risk for later reoccurrence or another kind of cancer. Doing things to improve your immune system would be helpful.

Being a cancer survivor can make you a hypochondriac. Every bump and unexplainable pain inside your body raises the question of cancer again. It happened once before, so it can happen again with a greater likelihood because of the treatment. This means regular checkups are important, and timely examinations should occur when suspicious problems arise. Keeping a record of self-examinations is also important. For example, note the time that changes are observed and the rate at which the change is progressing.

Confidence builds as time passes. This is a rather peculiar attitude because the more time that passes, the more likely you are to have cancer again. But for someone who has already had cancer, reaching the five-year mark is a big deal because the likelihood of cancer reoccurring diminishes.

Statistics are used to show generally what people experience, but statistics do not explain the individual differences. As I mentioned earlier, people have different experiences. Symptoms differ. Age, gender, health, genetics, and diet all contribute to the ways people experience symptoms during and after having cancer. Also, people respond differently to the same treatments. Statistics are numbers, not people.

My experience of having cancer was in the context of praying to understand Mark 11:22–23. God answered my prayer with an experience of stage 4 cancer. I did not pray for this particular mountain. I did not pray for the experience of suffering. I prayed to understand prayer. I was thinking more along the lines of studying about prayers that move mountains rather than being given a mountain to move for personal, firsthand knowledge.

MOUNTAINS AND MIRACLES

It was a miracle to be fully recovered from stage 4 Hodgkin's lymphoma and the chemotherapy. The timing for the diagnosis of my cancer one week after the completion of my study on prayer and specifically Mark 11:22–23, the tremendous success of the chemo, the amazing recovery of my health, the experience of God's presence and reassurance, and the beating of odds all confirmed that God had granted my desire to learn more about prayers that move mountains.

I recovered quickly. Life normalized. This experience was a chapter added to my life. I was surprised how quickly the experience seemed like a minor inconvenience and distraction. In just a couple of years, memory of it began to fade. I think the intensity of the experience may have been blunted by God's presence and comfort as well as the understanding that He was answering my prayer. God had His arms around Colleen and me with reassurance that was truly amazing. We could not have walked away from Him if we had wanted to. His love and presence were with us. He gave me my mountain, I learned, my prayer was granted, and now it was time to move on.

GREAT INSIGHTS TO REMEMBER

1. It is an insult to God not to use our brains and not to live more intelligently today than yesterday.
2. When we use our God-given intelligence, we are blessed.
3. All human intelligence and achievements are a testimony to the intelligent design of God's creation.
4. God will never contradict His Word, so anything known by faith will not violate God's written instructions.
5. God wants us to learn as much as we can about His creation and use that knowledge.
6. Admitting and confessing guilt for being sinful is difficult for many people, but it must be done to enjoy the blessings of eternal life.
7. If you accept the fact that you will inevitably die and perhaps sooner than you expect, you know you should prepare for death.
8. It would be nice to leave an encouraging letter that could be found someday by loved ones after you die.

5
A BIGGER MOUNTAIN

*If ye have faith as a grain of mustard seed,
nothing shall be impossible unto you.*
— Matthew 17:20

After finishing my chemo treatments in 1989, I was feeling great in no time. I was exercising regularly, leading the collegiate ministry, pastoring, training ministry team leaders, conducting creation science seminars, leading discipleship conferences, and teaching weekly Bible studies.

As the five-year anniversary of remission drew near, Colleen and I talked about celebrating the success of my recovery. A couple of weeks before the five-year anniversary, I detected a suspicious lump.

During a canoe trip on the Mulberry River with the collegiate ministry, I was helping a couple of girls with their canoe after they got stuck on the embankment of the river in a wooded area. I yanked on the main branch that was pinning the canoe in the mud, and it released suddenly. The end of the branch stabbed me in the middle of my left hip, and it was very painful. It seemed unusual to me that it hurt so much. The end of the branch was not very sharp, so I figured it must have hit a nerve. That evening, I noticed that the area of pain was bruised and discolored. A trail of blood discoloration under the skin went down to my knee. As I pushed on the area, it was not painful, but there was something massive inside my hip area. It was solid. At first I thought I had a hernia. But it was too hard. I was hopeful that it would go away, but after a week of waiting, it was still there. I went to see Dr. Hayward for a checkup.

As I lay on the examination table, Dr. Hayward poked around on me and then said shaking his head, "Oh no." I asked him what that meant. He looked at me and said, "We're going to have to do it all over again." I asked him to be more specific. What exactly were we going to do again? He said, "The cancer has returned."

He told me to get off the table and follow him to the radiology building next door. As we walked, we talked about how the treatment would be different for the second go-around. He told me that I would have to use the MOPP treatment. This is the more caustic chemo regimen that I wanted to avoid. I was feeling very apprehensive about this.

The x-ray confirmed that the lymph nodes in the left inguinal region were swollen. A follow-up biopsy confirmed Hodgkin's lymphoma. The doctor said that staging was unnecessary. The course of treatment would involve the full dose of MOPP drugs for the chemotherapy.

I had to make calls again to tell folks that the cancer had

returned. It was hardest to tell my parents. It was a painful and sorrowful conversation with my mom. She called the rest of the family for me. My church family and friends found out through our prayer chain.

I began to review literature for the latest research and treatments of Hodgkin's lymphoma as I had done before. But I discovered that there were not enough survivors for a five-year survival statistic. Cancer cells that survive chemotherapy repopulate as resistant cells. This means that a new regimen of chemo drugs or a higher dose of chemo drugs would have to be used to kill the new growth of resistant cells. I stopped reading articles and just prayed. My hope would be in God. I relaxed with a sense of relief, yet I had a curiosity about what God would do this time.

A FIERY TRIAL

During the five years after the first set of chemo treatments, I was very active. The doctor said he was amazed at my energy level. I was so active it was easy to forget that I had even been through a serious battle for my life.

Reoccurrence was not on my mind. I was over and done with cancer mentally and emotionally. It is interesting how much my thinking had changed. During the recovery period after treatments were finished, I had been thinking the chemo was not so bad. I had talked to God about how the chemo treatments did not seem to be too terribly difficult. The whole experience had been more of an inconvenience than a traumatic crisis. I'd had to keep reminding myself that the diagnosis was stage 4 Hodgkin's lymphoma. I remember thinking that it seemed too easy even though the survival statistics favored my demise. But God had answered my prayers and had walked with me through the experience to teach me about prayer.

> *I did not want to go through it again. This was a bigger mountain requiring a bigger miracle to survive.*

Now that I was faced with going through chemo again to battle cancer, the negative memories were returning. I prepared myself mentally and emotionally again for the experience. This time, I knew I was going into a fiery trial. Spiritually, I was praying and trusting the Lord. He was in control, and that was a fact that reassured me a great deal. But the experience was going to be tough. The first experience no longer seemed a trifle. I was remembering more of the unpleasant times. I did not want to go through it again. This was a bigger mountain requiring a bigger miracle to survive.

I was dreading the second round of treatment so much that I asked the church to pray for me about my attitude. It was the first time since I had been saved that I was fighting a battle in myself to cheerfully accept God's will. I was not afraid of God. I trusted Him and wanted His will to be done at all times. I did not want to miss out on the opportunities He had planned for me. But the thought of enduring another eight months of chemo was very unsettling.

One of the other patients being treated for Hodgkin's lymphoma in 1989 stopped his chemo treatments because it was so unpleasant. He chose quality of life and early death as a preferred option to the chemo. Many cancer patients face this dilemma at some point when the effects of chemo ruin their quality of life. Some are convinced that there is no point in enduring the side-effects if there is no hope of recovery. But for me, I had hope in Christ. He was still teaching me about prayer.

For me, dying was not worrisome. I was in God's hands. I could not imagine giving up, no matter the experience of the treatment. I dealt with my dread of the chemo quickly. When things are not right, I like to correct them as soon as I can. So I prepared myself mentally and spiritually to go through the fiery trial again. The thought of resisting God's will was more averse to me than the effects of chemo.

Put into perspective, my experience was nothing compared to Christ's experience on the cross. No suffering can compare to what Jesus experienced. Jesus endured incomprehensible suffering for our sins. And though He was God and had a perfect relationship with His Father, the anticipation of His suffering created enormous stress on Him. Luke 22:44 says, "And being in an agony he prayed more earnestly: and his sweat was as it were great drops of blood falling down to the ground." Yes, He knew He would rise again. He knew that He would conquer death. But what He would have to experience to pay for all the sins of all humanity would be infinitely excruciating. The anticipation of the suffering was agonizing for Him.

ENDURING CHEMO AGAIN

The treatments to fight the reoccurrence of cancer began in a new clinic that I had never been in before. Dr. Hayward now had a team of two other oncologists working with him. The clinic was bigger, and there were more patients in the waiting room. There were two rows of chairs for patients to sit in during treatments. There were more nurses attending patients. The only thing that had not changed was the smell of the betadine and alcohol. I had my mints with me.

> *The thought of resisting God's will was more averse to me than the effects of chemo.*

Two of the drugs needed to be delivered intravenously, so I had another port-a-cath sewn into my chest. The nitrogen mustard was the drug I dreaded the most. Stories of World War I came to mind, when mustard gas was used as a lethal weapon. It destroys tissue and mucous on contact. Oncovin, also known as Vincristine, was the second drug administered intravenously. The Procarbazine and prednisone were given in pill form and were taken orally. Prednisone is a steroid used to reduce inflammation and allergic reactions caused by the other drugs. Procarbazine is an anti-cancer drug that has a warning on it not to expose family members to it. Why? Because Procarbazine is also carcinogenic, so it is dangerous to expose others to it. Once again, I felt like my body was a toxic waste dump. The drugs used to kill cancer cells also increase the risk of converting normal cells into cancer cells. After using MOPP, about twenty percent of patients develop other cancers within twenty years.

I had a hard time swallowing pills because my gag reflex was so sensitive due to the nausea they caused. But it had to be done, so I put a pill on my tongue and filled my mouth with water to make it go down. They did not go down easily, and to this day my gag reflex is very sensitive. I can still taste and feel the sensation of those pills from over twenty-five years ago.

Since my first round of treatments five years earlier, a new anti-nausea drug called Zofran was on the market. It made it possible for me to drive myself to the clinic, and I didn't need to be knocked out with Ativan. All I did was sniff mint, especially while the betadine was wiped on my chest. All these years later, even the thought of betadine makes me feel sick.

PREPARING FOR DEATH AGAIN

With the prospect of my not being around for Colleen and Lisa again, we had to review our preparation for my demise. But we also had our second daughter, Tenille, who was born August 1992. I joked that there seemed to be a pattern developing. I told Colleen that we would have to stop having children because it was killing me. But Tenille was our miracle baby. The doctor had told us that we should not expect to have another child after the chemotherapy in 1989. When we discovered that we would have another baby, we celebrated.

I was preparing for my demise because statistically it was very likely. I was confident about being in the Lord's hands, just like the first time around. In fact, I was sort of looking forward to what the Lord was going to take me through. But I felt that it would be very irresponsible not to take care of my family. I had mixed emotions. I was fully trusting the Lord and perfectly at peace with His will but was dreading the experience of chemo with the MOPP drugs. And the second time around was a painful experience.

THE SECOND TIME WORSE THAN THE FIRST

The second round of treatments was similar to the first in that I went in every other week. I was facing death's door and heaven's gates as I went through chemo all over again. As before, the first week after each treatment my health declined. The second week was for rebounding. With all of the chemo being put in me, I felt like a walking poison sack. Also, just like the first time, I saw ugly images when I closed my eyes. They were like looking at a framed relief sculpture of vague, mud-gray, worm-like features. The sight of them made me feel nauseous.

After each treatment, the waves of nausea, headaches, insomnia, digestive shutdown, cramping, bloating, and fatigue continued for about nine days. The symptoms increased in intensity with each treatment. Dr Hayward was giving me the maximum dosage. After each treatment, I was weaker and sicker than the previous treatment.

One day, my pastor came by to visit and brought a Korean friend who was studying at the University of Arkansas. After our conversation, we knelt down to pray. Afterwards, I had to ask the pastor to help me up because I could not get my legs to push me up. On another occasion, walking down a small flight of stairs, I stumbled as my legs gave out. My favorite position at home was lying down. It was a perfect position for the strength I had in me.

Each chemo treatment had at least one unique symptom associated with it. From hearing the pounding of my heartbeat in my ears to nosebleeds, joint aches, elevated heart rate, and rashes, every week there was something new happening.

> *From hearing the pounding of my heartbeat to nosebleeds, joint aches, elevated heart rate, and rashes, every week there was something new happening.*

The most painful experience occurred when my mouth felt like it was filled with habanero peppers. About two days after the fourth treatment, a fiery heat began inside my upper cheeks and gums on both sides of my mouth. Each day, the pain progressed a little farther down the inside of my cheeks, then across the roof of my mouth, and under my tongue. Then fiery pain was on my tongue. The following day it went down my throat. The pain was excruciating. The doctor examined my mouth but saw no indication of thrush or any other fungal infection, blistering, or exfoliation. The cause was not apparent, but the pain was very real. The doctor gave me lidocaine, but that did not help. The pain prevented me from sleeping or doing anything other than trying to find some relief by holding ice water in my mouth. A friend at church suggested that I try using Hurricane spray. It is used to numb the gums of babies who are teething. One shot of spray, and I felt relief. Every five minutes, I was spraying my mouth with Hurricane. I was so grateful for the relief. Who would have guessed that a numbing medication for babies' gums would give me relief?

As much as I was seeking relief from the burning pain in my mouth, I still can't imagine how excruciating the pain must have been for the rich man in hell. In Luke 16, Jesus tells the story of a man named Lazarus. This was a different Lazarus from the man Jesus raised from the dead. This Lazarus was a very poor man who every day sat by the house gate of a very wealthy man. Eventually, both died. Lazarus ended up in heaven with Abraham. The rich man ended up in the fires of hell. Salvation is not determined by your success in this life, your wealth, or your fame. Salvation has nothing to do with your personal accomplishments or abilities. It is all about what Jesus does. It is all about God's mercy and grace. It is about God's promise to those who simply trust Him rather than trust themselves.

While in hell, the rich man was able to look across what is described as a great expanse separating heaven from hell. The fact that Lazarus was named is a good indication this was not a parable, but a real account. The rich man saw Lazarus and Abraham at a distance, "and he cried and said, Father Abraham, have mercy on me, and send Lazarus, that he may dip the tip of his finger in water, and cool my tongue; for I am tormented in this flame" (Luke 16:24). The pain this rich man experienced was far greater than what I experienced, but I can sympathize with the need for relief. At least I found relief. Sadly, there is no relief in hell and no hope of ever getting relief.

Another difficulty I endured occurred about three months into the chemotherapy. I was struggling physically. I was too weak to climb stairs, and the muscles in my legs were cramping day and night. My heart was pounding so loud in my ears that it was distracting me from hearing other things for two weeks straight. And I had difficulty controlling bleeding from my nose.

My diary entry from that time says, "Resting heart rate Monday morning was 90 beats/minute. After walking 25 feet, it was 100/min. After a shower, it was 110/min. I have been on the verge of exhaustion for five days. I count my pulse by listening to it in my ears, which is convenient because I cannot use my fingers to feel anything. They are too numb. Any activity wears me out. I can sit in a backless chair for about four minutes. Dizzy spells accompany every activity. A dull ache is present above the center of my diaphragm. Sharper pains occur when I eat. I am always out of breath though all I am doing is lying here in bed."

The headaches intensified, but the sinus mucous was clear. My heart was racing consistently at over 100 beats per minute. There was constant pressure in my ears, a steady pounding of my heart, and I had a loud ringing in my ears. The doctor said that he could see a little fluid building up in my ears. But there was no fever. Nonetheless, he prescribed Sulfamethoxazole for me to fight a possible infection. I was wondering if the oxygen deficiency were causing the headaches and rapid heart rate. I was praying for relief, and after weeks of misery I began to feel better. My toes and fingers were still numb, but the intensity of the pains subsided.

With my face buried in the sheets and too exhausted to move, I asked God for help. Immediately, I was covered with the presence of God.

After a later treatment, my health declined again. I could barely turn over in bed. With my face buried in the sheets and too exhausted to move, I asked God for help. Immediately, I was covered with the presence of God. I felt reassured and comforted by His presence. It was a tremendous experience.

Due to the debilitating effects of the chemo, a couple of treatments were postponed in the schedule to accommodate Christmas and New Year's Day. That way I was able to eat food and enjoy the celebrations on my good weeks.

Then in January, after a treatment, my health declined quickly.

I was barely able to get out of bed. When I did, I sat in the big, fluffy reclining chair in the living room. I was exhausted from the walk to the living room. I wasn't eating. I was barely drinking and was miserable. My ears were hearing the pounding of my heart, my head hurt, my eyesight was blurry, and my heart rate was over a hundred beats per minute. My stomach and intestines were inflamed and swollen. I was hoping that the chemo was working twice as well on the cancer cells as it was on the rest of me. When I looked in the mirror, I looked pasty, pale white. I pulled my eyelids down, and there was no color in them.

It was a Sunday in January when I was forced to make a difficult decision. Colleen was getting ready to go to church that evening, and I was debating all day whether to tell her how bad I really felt. I was concerned that she might come home and find me dead. I debated what to do all afternoon. Then before she left, I asked her if she ever thought about what she would do if she found me in the chair not breathing. It was a good question to think about anyway. What would you do?

All I could do was lie in bed or sit in a chair. I could not even take a shower. I was exhausted doing nothing. I lost awareness of how my body was doing. I stopped trying to understand what I was feeling and why. There were too many variables to consider from diet, to bone marrow damage from the chemo, to indigestion, to organ failure, and so on.

My journal entry from that time says, "Sunday morning my skin turned pale gray and leathery, my saliva was foamy, all color in my face was gone, and I was stuck in bed due to exhaustion with a resting heart rate of 100/min. I have been on a liquid diet for five meals (soup, Ensure, juice). I drank water and a gallon of apple juice Sunday."

Colleen went to church in tears. She told a good friend of mine what I had said to her, and he came to visit me after church. He had just completed medical school and was doing his residency in the area, so I was fortunate to have him around. He examined me and said that I was lacking blood and was in need of a blood transfusion.

The problem with blood transfusions in the 1980s and early 1990s was that political correctness had crept into the scientific and medical communities. The Centers for Disease Control (CDC) and the American Red Cross were sending blood mobiles to high risk communities without proper screening techniques for HIV. A sheriff in Fort Smith, Arkansas, who had been shot, received a blood transfusion to save his life and then died from an HIV infection he received from contaminated blood given to him.

> I was appalled by the lack of common sense and professionalism shown by people who should know better.

Being in the field of microbiology, I was appalled by the lack of common sense and professionalism shown by people who should know better. When the first outbreak of AIDS became news in 1981, there was concern in the medical community about avoiding a widespread public panic and backlash against the homosexual community. The CDC and news media jumped on the political bandwagon, telling people that AIDS was not a disease exclusive to the homosexual communities. That was correct. But the statistics from the CDC, reporting that over 94 percent of AIDS cases were from the male homosexual community, were censored.

AIDS was an unknown disease at the time, and nobody knew what caused the disease or how it was transmitted. HIV was not identified as the cause of AIDS until 1984. Yet many healthcare professionals assured the public that AIDS was an STD that was not easily transmitted. When I questioned how the CDC and medical experts could tell people they couldn't get a disease when they didn't know what caused it, I got some condemning looks from others in the microbiology department. Obviously, being in the science field does not make one immune to the politics of the day. The way the CDC and the American Red Cross and other medical groups dealt with the HIV problem was reckless and irresponsible.

So I told the doctor I was not taking any risks by using the community blood supply. After all this effort to fight for my life, I was not going to use the blood supplies of the American Red Cross and the CDC. But to use my own blood would take six days, and I did not have six days. And I did not have blood to put into storage anyway. What was I to do?

One of our church members put out an announcement on our prayer chain that I needed safe, screened blood. Twenty-two men from the church volunteered. I had more than enough blood donated for my need.

In preparing for the transfusion at the hospital, I asked some of the men to rotate on a thirty-minute to one-hour time schedule so that I would have someone in the room with me while Colleen was at work. I was not doing well and did not know if I would be conscious, so I wanted someone to be in the room to oversee what was going on. Fortunately, I was conscious.

My concern and being wary of mistakes and carelessness in the hospital were confirmed by one incident. One of the techs came from the lab to prepare me for the transfusion and wheeled his tray next to the bed. I looked at what he had laid out on the tray and noticed that he did not have the right equipment for accessing a port-a-cath. I told him that I had a port, and he ignored me while continuing to prepare his materials. I told him again that I had a port and that the needles he had would not work. He grunted and said he understood. I told him again, but he never looked at me. He barely acknowledged what I was saying. So I just sat in bed waiting for him to finish whatever he was doing.

Then he said, "Okay, let's do this," holding the needle and rubber tubing in his hand. I pulled back my shirt to reveal my port, watched his face, and said nothing. Only then did he realize his mistake. He said he couldn't do the procedure with the needle he had. I told him I knew that. Another tech was sent from the lab, and the blood transfusion went smoothly.

Being the patient does not mean that you resign your health and wellbeing to the medical staff.

Being the patient does not mean that you resign your health and well-being to the medical staff. They are there to help you. But you need to make sure that someone who knows you is present to care for you if you cannot care for yourself. If you don't, unnecessary mistakes can happen.

The transfusion went smoothly. But the nurse was shocked that I needed four units of blood and was surprised that I was still walking. It took two days for me to get all the needed blood. The chemo treatments were preventing my body from producing enough red blood cells (RBC) and white blood cells (WBC) on its own. The doctor postponed another couple of treatments because my blood cell counts were too low. But there were new drugs called leukopoietin and erythropoietin that were just coming into use that could help boost the production of the cells. My WBC count was very low at about 100 cells/ul. But a few days after an injection with leukopoietin, my WBC was over 30,000. Normal is about 12,000. With the use of these two blood boosting drugs, I was able to complete the remainder of the treatments.

REMISSION AND POST TREATMENT

After eight months of chemo, all tests showed once again that the cancer was gone. A spot in one of my lymph nodes was still present, but the doctor thought it was scar tissue.

After completing the chemo, I worked on recovering my strength and health. I ate well and exercised. It took a little longer than the first time, but I was fully engaged every day doing something.

At the time of writing this book in 2019, my activity level and health are as good as ever. I have been cancer free for over twenty-five years. It has been thirty-one years since my first battle with cancer. If cancer strikes again, I will continue to put my trust in the Lord.

I have forgotten a lot of things that took place during my chemotherapy, so I am glad for the notes I wrote and for Colleen and friends to remind me.

The chemotherapeutic drugs given to me are known to cause memory loss. One evening, while reading, I told Colleen I thought I had read the book before. I write reviews of some of the books I read, so I looked through my files, and sure enough, I had written a review of the book I was reading. That was very discouraging. My ability to think and reason was intact, but my memory was suffering. I stopped reading for about a year. I wasn't remembering what I read anyway. I talked to the doctor about the problem, and he told me that it was possible that the drugs had affected my memory. Then he added with a smile, "And you are getting older." Age and drugs were affecting my memory. I began reading tips on how to improve memory, and of course, crossword puzzles were mentioned. I hate crosswords, but the newspaper always had Sudoku puzzles, so I began doing those. Within a week, I noticed a dramatic improvement. I still have difficulty with short-term memory, but it has significantly improved.

Because everyone inevitably dies, cancer survival, like with other fatal diseases, is described in terms of average lifespan. Some die sooner, and some later.

The question is not if you will die, but when. It is important to prepare for death, not to dwell on it, but to accept it as part of life. Live life fully, set big goals, and make your life count by living for the Lord. Confirm that you are saved, and think about the spiritual needs of others. Being heaven-bound is the only way to exit this life on Earth.

> The question is not if you will die, but when.

As I age, my body continues to deteriorate, as does anyone's body over time. My eyes do not work as well as they used to. I don't swim forty laps in the pool anymore. I have had surgeries on my thyroid and a titanium plate screwed into my neck. This is life.

Death is a part of life. God tells us to expect it and to prepare for it. James 1:11 says, "For the sun is no sooner risen with a burning heat, but it withereth the grass, and the flower thereof falleth, and the grace of the fashion of it perisheth: so also shall the rich man fade away in his ways." Generations after generations rise and fall away over time. Wealth, knowledge, and ability cannot prevent death.

Luke 12:19–21 tells of a man who failed to prepare for his death. The man says to himself, "…Soul, thou hast much goods laid up for many years; take thine ease, eat, drink, and be merry. But God said unto him, Thou fool, this night thy soul shall be required of thee: then whose shall those things be, which thou hast provided? So is he that layeth up treasure for himself, and is not rich toward God."

Life is much more than what we do on Earth. Life is about enjoying a relationship with God, our Creator and Savior of the world, Jesus Christ. Many spend their time and talents preparing for retirement and death. But God tells us to prepare for life everlasting. Life does not have to end with physical death. Life can continue forever in heaven with God. With God's perspective, rather than live with a sense of impending doom anticipating your demise, you can live with hope of eternal life. Everyone must still pass through the door of physical death, but many will enter into the eternal, heavenly presence of God. Will you?

Isaiah 40:8 says that "the grass withereth, the flower fadeth: but the word of our God shall stand for ever." Our physical bodies are temporary, and death is inevitable, but eternal life is guaranteed by God's promise. Hebrews 6:17–18 declares, "Wherein God, willing more abundantly to shew unto the heirs of promise the immutability of his counsel, confirmed it by an oath: That by two immutable things, in which it was impossible for God to lie, we might have a strong consolation, who have fled for refuge to lay hold upon the hope set before us." God's promise and God's oath guarantee eternal life to anyone and everyone who believe on Him. And unlike this earth and heaven, we will be blessed with "… an inheritance incorruptible, and undefiled, and that fadeth not away, reserved in heaven for you" (First Peter 1:4).

PREPARING FOR ROUND THREE

The doctor told me that it would be a good idea to harvest my bone marrow cells after recovering from the chemo in case the cancer returned. The lack of survivors in my circumstance strongly indicated that I should expect the cancer to return within five years, and that survival was unlikely past five years.

I went to Little Rock for the harvest. Sixty-five plugs would be taken out of my hips, so I was put under anesthesia. I woke up with two big patches on my back, one on each side of my hip bones. The doctor told me it would feel like someone kicked me with steel-toed boots. It was painful but was more like a dull ache. Healing and improvement from the marrow harvest were noticeable each day, much like a bruise heals. A week later, I was walking without pain. The harvested bone cells were stored in a refrigerator.

Most statistics use a five-year mark to measure the probability of cancer reoccurring. There is also the prospect of other cancers developing due to the exposure to radiation and carcinogenic chemicals during treatment. In my case, there was a high probability of developing a cancer or having organ failure within twenty years after the chemo treatment with MOPP. But thirty years have now passed since my first set of treatments. I've been cancer free for twenty-five years since my reoccurrence. The Lord has preserved me for a longer period of time to serve Him.

If the cancer had returned within five years, the only recourse would have been to do a bone marrow transplant. The procedure is not pleasant. It involves killing the bone marrow cells in your body with an intense dosage of chemotherapy and radiation. Your bone marrow is where blood cells and immune cells are produced. From start to finish, it may take about thirty days. By killing the bone marrow, residual cancer cells hiding in the marrow are killed. Then, by means of a blood transfusion, clean bone cells are dripped back into the body where they reseed themselves in the marrow.

This is a dangerous procedure because without bone marrow, your immune system is severely compromised. You are vulnerable to being infected by germs. Between the time your bone marrow is killed and the time it takes for your new bone marrow to be established, you are not able to protect yourself from infections.

LESSONS LEARNED

The bigger the mountain, the bigger the miracle. God answered my prayers to understand mountain-moving prayers by giving me two big mountains to move. In hindsight, the experiences were tremendous. God did grant my prayers. He took me through fiery trials, but He was with me. He taught me about prayer with experience as well as with His Word.

It seems to me that during my trials I learned more than I was aware of. I know that I changed, but I cannot describe all the ways I changed. All I can say is that I am better off because of prayers and because of God's answers. Likewise, your prayers and God's answers will make you better too. The answers may not be the same, but the benefits will be no less if you put your trust in Him.

GREAT INSIGHTS TO REMEMBER

1. Hope in God brings peace and relief to the grieving heart.
2. Trusting in God does not mean suffering will not occur.
3. Suffering should be expected in a world plagued with sin. Christ came and suffered.
4. Being in God's will creates a sense of anticipation for what He has planned.
5. No pain on earth compares to the pain and sorrow of those in hell.
6. The wise are motivated by pain and sorrow now to avoid future pain and suffering.
7. Death is inevitable. Preparing for your exit will determine where you spend eternity.

6
PRAY WELL

Continue in prayer, and watch in the same with thanksgiving.
— Colossians 4:2

God granted my request to understand prayers that move mountains. I am very grateful that the lesson went beyond reading and thinking about prayer. He gave me a mountain to pray about. I prayed; He moved it. Prayer is not about our power to control God. It is about what God can do for us.

I do not just talk about prayer. I have experienced prayer that moves mountains. And yet I feel very deficient in my understanding and practice of prayer. Nonetheless, I am happy to share what I have learned.

If you have any doubt about the benefit of prayer, I hope my testimony encourages you to pray. God is real, and He is powerful.

> *Prayer is not about our power to control God. It is about what God can do for us.*

Nothing is impossible for God. My testimony is about what God did for me. His answer may be different for you, but He will always answer you. The question is will you always hear Him and listen to Him?

My prayer is that your life has improved after reading this book and that your outlook on life is more hopeful. It is my prayer that your life is so fulfilling that you enjoy praying and that you look forward to sharing lessons about prayer with others. The Lord answered my request to be taught about prayer. Will your experience be similar?

Following are seven lessons mentioned in my testimony about prayer that I find noteworthy.

SEVEN NOTEWORTHY LESSONS

1. Prayer is just a conversation with God.
2. There is always hope in any and every situation when you are following God's will.
3. Being saved by God is the first step to praying prayers that move mountains.
4. Faith, belief, and righteousness are the minimum requirements for praying correctly.
5. Faith is not belief. Faith is what you believe in.
6. There are four types of prayers.
7. God answers every prayer, with the ultimate goal of saving souls.

Jesus Christ is the reason there is hope in prayer. He hears, and He answers. In this book, I have described the hope we can have because of prayer. In my book *PRAY: How God Answers Every Prayer,* I explain how prayer works and how to pray the prayers that avail much. I describe insights into how to pray prayers that are granted and how to recognize God's answers to every prayer. Learning how to pray right is very rewarding and thrilling.

LEARN MORE ABOUT PRAYER

Learning about prayer is like living. There is always more to learn. There are always new experiences. Second Timothy 2:15 says, "Study to shew thyself approved unto God, a workman that needeth not to be ashamed, rightly dividing the word of truth." Study the prayers of Jesus. Think about the prayers of Paul. Study all the Bible verses that teach about prayer. Ask God to teach you more about prayer.

Follow the example of prayers mentioned in the Bible. For example, read Paul's explanation of how he prays. In Philippians 1:9–11, he says, "And this I pray, that your love may abound yet more and more in knowledge and in all judgment; That ye may approve things that are excellent; that ye may be sincere and without offence till the day of Christ; Being filled with the fruits of righteousness, which are by Jesus Christ, unto the glory and praise of God." In this case, we discover a little about how Paul prayed for others. His prayer serves as an example of how we can pray too.

Read and pray through David's prayers in the book of Psalms. David sang many of his prayers. Remember that prayer is talking to God. Sing to Him if you wish. Read through the prayers of David, and discover how to pray to God as you follow his thoughts to guide you in your own prayers. The important thing is that you communicate to God. You do not need to script out your prayers. You do not need to chant the same phrase repeatedly. God is not impressed by repetition of memorized, scripted words and phrases. He wants you to talk to Him. He wants you to genuinely express yourself.

If you are frustrated or disappointed about something in your prayer life, talk to God about it. Ask Him to teach you and to answer your questions. Do not be too shy to ask. God already knows what you are thinking and feeling. Talk to God about whatever is on your mind. If you are struggling with a bad thought, tell Him you know it is a bad thought, and ask Him to help you think and feel right.

Participate in prayer groups, especially your church meetings, to learn from others. Listen to what others are praying about. Ask them questions about their prayer lives. Don't just listen to the prayers of others. Pray silently as others pray. Group prayer is a group discussion with God.

SHARE YOUR LESSONS ABOUT PRAYER

I want to encourage you to share your favorite lessons about prayer with others. This is what Paul and the apostles did. And as the Christians in the early church participated in group prayers, many were learning by example of how to pray.

Acts 2:42 describes the practice of Christians, saying, "And they continued stedfastly in the apostles' doctrine and fellowship, and in breaking of bread, and in prayers." They assembled together, they shared the teachings of the apostles, they fellowshipped, they ate together, and they prayed together.

Are you a part of a church fellowship that assembles for training, fellowship, worship, and prayer? This is the example for us to follow. Hebrews 10:25 says, "Not forsaking the assembling of ourselves together, as the manner of some is; but exhorting one another: and so much the more, as ye see the day approaching."

We need to learn from others, and we need to be sharing our lessons with others. It is in sharing and teaching that we gain in understanding.

I'd like to hear from you. If this book has been a blessing to you, please visit my website at patrickbriney.com to share your story.

- Share your favorite thought or lesson from the book.
- Share how your prayer life improved because of lessons learned.
- Sign up for the online course, and learn even more about prayer.

BE DELIBERATE

The spirit is willing, but the flesh is weak. So your inclination will be to postpone your prayers until a later time. Don't do it. Be intentional and make your prayers happen, even if it is on the road driving to work. Like eating, there is always time to pray. No man ever starved for lack of time to eat.

Make it happen. Don't make excuses. If you are struggling with a lack of motivation to pray, remember, the quality of your prayer life is a reflection of the quality of your relationship with God. The confidence you have in prayer reflects the confidence you have in God.

Right now is a good time to pray. Hopefully, you have been praying and applying the lessons learned as you have been reading this book. And I pray that you will share these lessons with others as well.

Pray for everything and anything that you think would be pleasing to God. Ask Him about other desires you have. He might grant those too. Be persistent and consider fasting for the more difficult requests.

Set aside special time. Pray for specific things in addition to generalities. Focus your attention on praying to God, not on words and repetitious phrases. Be prayerful all the time. Constant prayer means developing awareness of God at all times. If you sense God is with you all the time, you can pray to Him anytime.

SETTING PRIORITIES

What are the most important things in life? When faced with the prospect of death, you realize quickly what is really important.

For me, it was God, family, and friends. My relationship with God is of utmost importance because it determines my eternal destiny. My relationship with my family is fulfilling, which is by divine design. My relationship with my church family and friends is satisfying. These are not the only things, but they are the most important.

Obviously, people live without a decent relationship with God, family, or friends. Existence is all some can imagine. Some despair of what they are missing. Others cope as best they can by ignoring their loss, denying the loss, or accepting the loss. People for the most part are survivors in the sense of making do with what they have. But there is so much more to enjoy in life. This is what God wants for us. This is what God's plan is for us. This is what life will be like for those who enter heaven with Him where there will be no sin.

People make life harder on themselves than is necessary. They spoil their relationship with God because of sin and selfishness. They spoil their family relationships because of selfishness and disrespect. They spoil their friendships because of the same. God's way is so much better.

There are many demands in our lives that need attention. Which demands are most important? Some use a strict list of priorities to help them make choices. You have probably seen the list that begins with God, then family, and then country. It sounds good, but a priority *list* is fundamentally flawed. As long as there is a second priority, there is always a competitor to number one. This means that you always have something in your life that is competing with God as your top priority. And sometimes, the list becomes very impractical when trying to live by it. After all, how do you measure a priority in time or quality of time?

Priority Circle

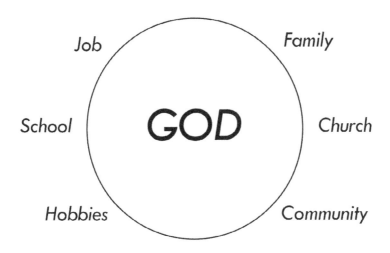

To resolve this unnecessary conflict and competition of priorities, I resort to using a circle rather than a list to describe how best to live for God and to get everything done properly. With God in the middle of the circle and everything else listed on the perimeter of the circle, an important perspective is reinforced, namely, that God is first, second, third, etc. He *is* the priority. Everything done should be done for Him. Turning your attention to your family, friends, job, school, career, hobbies, and so forth, is not forsaking God or compromising your commitment to Him. Rather, whatever you do, you do all for God and because of God.

The perimeter of the circle shows what is important to you in the context of living for God. If there is something on the priority circle that is not honoring to God or is distracting you from honoring God in other things, remove it from your life.

The priority circle is more practical than a list. It is more representative of how people live. Everything on the circle is important and needs attention. The only way to honor God is to give *sufficient* attention to each thing on your circle. And at different times, the focus will be on one thing. This is how my life is. Nothing stays the same, but everything is important. Sometimes I call this circle the squeaky wheel because the squeakier things on the circle get more attention at the time but are still no more important than the other things on the circle.

First Corinthians 10:31 is the life verse that God impressed on me shortly after I was saved. It says, "Whether therefore ye eat, or drink, or whatsoever ye do, do all to the glory of God." This verse has always been prominent in my thinking about how to live life.

The most important thing you can do is help someone else improve their relationship with God, and prayer is a good way to do that. There is no relationship with God without prayer.

THOUGHTS TO ENCOURAGE YOU

- God still moves mountains.
- God can move mountains for you.
- God loves you.
- God sacrificed everything for your well-being.
- God is in control.
- God answers every prayer.

- God's answers are the best answers.
- All things work together for good to them who love Him.

GREAT INSIGHTS TO REMEMBER

1. Learn more about prayer.
2. Share what you learn about prayer with others.
3. Be deliberate to make prayer happen in your life.
4. You will only pray when prayer and God are important enough to you.
5. Faith, belief, and righteousness are the minimum requirements for prayers that avail.
6. Share in the answers to prayers by joining others who pray.
7. Learn from others to pray better.
8. Through prayer, be part of a spiritual movement throughout heaven and all of creation. Our God hears from where you are and grants answers where you are not.

EPILOGUE

According to the United States National Cancer Institute, cancer is the leading cause of death worldwide. It is estimated that almost forty percent of the U.S. population will be diagnosed with cancer during their lifetime. In 2018, over half a million people died from the disease.

Fortunately, my life is not determined by what happens to most people. Is yours? Life events do not have to happen to a person just because it usually happens a certain way to most people. Statistics represent general trends in the population. They do not represent individuals. Likewise, when God is involved, a person is no longer a statistic. Prayer changes things. It changed the story of my life.

The first time the doctor told me I had cancer, I was already in the fourth stage of lymphoma. The statistics for my survival were against me. After eight months of chemo, I was in remission. But five years later, I was told that the cancer had returned. I asked the doctor if he had ever treated a patient in my situation successfully. He said no.

I had prayed to understand the prayers that move mountains. God granted my request. He gave me a mountain. I did not pray for this mountain. He gave it to me to teach me what it takes to move it.

As a college student studying science, I learned through classroom instruction, laboratory demonstrations, and field experience. It is the proverbial triad of learning summed up in the anonymous statement: "I hear and I forget; I see and I remember; I do and I understand."

As a student of God's Word prayerfully seeking to understand prayers that produce consistent and predictable results including miracles, I unwittingly embarked on a journey of the learning triad. I studied the Bible to learn about prayer. I read in the Bible about the experiences of those who demonstrated mountain-moving prayers and observed those who claim to move mountains today. Then God took me into the laboratory of learning by experience.

I don't know about you, but I want to experience the blessings of God. My desire is to live for God. This goes beyond learning about God and learning about the Bible. For me, it is not enough to know about prayer or to talk about prayer. I want to experience it. I don't want to just talk about God. I want the experience of living with God in my life. I want to experience prayer. I want to understand it. And I thank Him for such experiences. I am humbled to share such experiences, not as one who knows all about prayer, but as one who knows a little more about prayer than when I first asked God to teach me.

Prayer, unlike any other discipline in the Christian walk, is a personal interaction with God. It is a daily, moment-by-moment, two-way communication with Him. The experience of powerful, successful prayers is not possible without a personal relationship with God. This requires being willing to fully and wholeheartedly trust Him and live for Him.

Learning by experience personalizes the insights gained and develops deep convictions. When you learn by experience, lessons become a part of your life for the rest of your life. James 1:22–25 explains it this way: "But be ye doers of the word, and not hearers only, deceiving your own selves. For if any be a hearer of the word, and not a doer, he is like unto a man beholding his natural face in a glass: For he beholdeth himself, and goeth his way, and straightway forgetteth what manner of man he was. But whoso looketh into the perfect law of liberty, and continueth therein, he being not a forgetful hearer, but a doer of the work, this man shall be blessed in his deed." Experience is learning by application. It is not easily forgotten.

I trusted the Lord as my Savior in February of 1977. I trusted Him with my life. I believed in Him and in His teachings. I wanted His will and plan for my life. I trusted Him to guide me through life. To this day, I continue to pray, "Lord, live your life through me. I am your willing vessel. Do as you please with my life. I confess, I am the weak link in understanding and application, but I am willing to do my best."

I determined to do all that I could to live for Him. I committed to do His will and to let Him do the rest. I wanted to say as the Apostle Paul said in Galatians 2:20, "I am crucified with Christ: nevertheless I live; yet not I, but Christ liveth in me: and the life which I now live in the flesh I live by the faith of the Son of God, who loved me, and gave himself for me."

I was eighteen years old when someone shared Galatians 2:20 with me for the first time. I was not a believer at the time. But I had asked my friend what made it possible for him as a Christian to live for God as he did. How was it possible to live as God wanted him to live? He told me it was Christ who lived in him. I remember I was amazed by the verse and by his explanation. If the verse were true, then there was a real-world experience of having God live in you. I wondered if it were really possible. If it were, then I wanted to experience it.

I am happy to share with you that the experience is real. And God has used my testimony to encourage and teach others to live for Christ and to pray better. I have been blessed by the experience.

The experience of having Christ live in me is very important to me. Though even on my best days I fall way short of being what Christ is, I pray for His will to be done, and He helps me do what I am able and willing to do.

Why do I seek this experience? I have this nagging curiosity to understand. I wonder what God could do with me if I were fully yielded to His will. And so I am compelled daily to surrender to Him with anticipation of His will for my life. I don't want to miss out on anything. I don't want to find out in heaven what could have been.

In heaven, I would rather find out what *would* have happened in my life if I had *not* prayed and surrendered to Him than to find out what *could* have been if I *had* prayed and surrendered to Him. Perhaps you are seeking this experience too. I hope this book will help.

I asked God many times to teach me by giving me instant understanding in order to bypass the lessons that come with experience. Although He does grant wisdom and insights by His Word and by faith, I have learned that He requires learning by experience as well. I still pray for instant understanding to save time, but the Lord says experience is required. Obviously, this must be the best way to learn, and one day God will show me why. I have no doubt that He will.

The thoughts and lessons in this book come from my personal experience. After a year of focused study of every verse I could find in the Bible about prayer, the Lord put me through the school of experience. He answered my prayers to understand prayer by including application and experience. I went from the classroom into the laboratory, then into the field for real world training.

I pray my personal study and experience will be helpful to you in your journey to learn and experience prayers that move mountains.

Most people are faced with a crisis in their lives at some time, or they know someone who is facing a crisis. Can prayer help? I know it can, and this book tells my story of prayer that works.

Many people are disappointed with prayer. They wonder why God doesn't help them as they ask. They struggle with the feeling that prayer is a waste of time. Does prayer really work? Does God really listen? How does God decide which prayers to grant?

You will be pleased to know that the information in this book is not the end. With a correct understanding of prayer, you will pray more, pray for more people, and pray more effectively. It is an exciting journey. I am convinced there is no end to learning more about prayer.

APPENDIX

MYTHS AND FACTS ABOUT PRAYER

1. MYTH: God is more likely to grant prayers that are memorized and repeated. FACT: God is not a machine that receives coins to make Him grant prayers.

2. MYTH: God is more likely to grant prayers that are said in the "best position." FACT: Men of God in the Bible pray standing, kneeling, and falling on their faces. They lift up their hands, they hold food, and sometimes, they do not lift their hands. Some close their eyes. Others do not. Some walk while praying.

3. MYTH: God does not hear the prayers of the lost nor the carnal Christian. FACT: God is right next to you. How can He not hear you?

4. MYTH: God grants all the prayer requests of godly Christians. FACT: God grants every prayer request that aligns with His will.

5. MYTH: Prayers prayed with more power are more powerful and more likely to be granted. FACT: The power is in God not in our prayers.

6. MYTH: Prayer should always be offered in the privacy of your personal closet. FACT: Public prayers and private prayers were a part of Israel's and the early churches' experiences. Praying in your closet means praying to God, not for the attention of others. This can be done in public as well as in private.

7. MYTH: Ultimately, prayer is not necessary because God will do what He wants to do anyway. FACT: James 4:2 says that you have not because you ask not. If prayer can change things, then failure to pray fails to change things that otherwise could have been changed. Further, God expects you to pray, which means it is necessary to pray.

8. MYTH: Claim a promise in the name of Jesus, and it will happen. FACT: God only does that which is according to His will, not your will.

FOURTEEN PRAYER INSIGHTS

1. We must pray in order to obey God.
2. Faith is the revelation of God's will.
3. Belief is your response to the revelation received from God.
4. Having a little faith refers to how much understanding you have about God's will.
5. If you believe what God reveals to you, it will come to pass,

and nothing can prevent it.

6. Intercessory prayers answered bless all those who pray for others.
7. God expects intercessory prayers to be part of the Christian experience.
8. In many cases, God requires prayer in order to make things happen.
9. God responds to prayers because of the needs we have.
10. Praying is an act of reliance on God.
11. Prayers do not change God's will; they change what He will do.
12. Just as Job could not persuade his friends due to their faulty thinking, God cannot persuade people who are blinded by faulty thinking.
13. Rather than complain about what God is not doing, we should be complaining about what we are doing.
14. Knowing that God always does what is best for us is essential to accepting all His answers.

TIPS TO PREPARE FOR MEDICAL APPOINTMENTS

- Prepare a list of specific questions that you want answered, and give them to the doctor during your visit. Sending the list to the physician in advance might be helpful.
- Be prepared to take notes. Bring a pencil and notebook to all meetings and examinations. Having someone with you is helpful.

- Take a list of your current prescriptions and any alternative medicine plans you might have.

SOME GENERAL QUESTIONS TO ASK THE DOCTOR

- What kind of cancer do I have?
- How far along is my cancer? (What stage is it?)
- What has been your experience with cancer patients like me?
- Should I get a second opinion?
- What are my treatment options?
- What treatments are best for me? Why?
- Why are you recommending this therapy? Is this standard procedure?
- What is the goal and prognosis for me? How successful have you been?
- Will I have to stay in the hospital for treatment? How long?
- Is treatment painful? How is pain managed?
- What are the side effects and treatments for them?
- How often will I be checked during and after treatment?
- Can I go back to normal daily activities after treatment?
- Are there any clinical trials that might be beneficial to me?
- Can you recommend any patient support groups in my area?
- What do you recommend that I do next? What can I do to help myself?
- Can chemotherapy ease my symptoms?
- How soon do you expect to see results?

- What side effects should I prepare for and how? What are the risks?
- What should I do to prepare for chemo treatments?
- How often will the treatments take place?
- Where do treatments take place?
- Will I be able to drive myself home after treatment, or do I need help?
- How long will each session of my chemotherapy treatments last? And how many sessions will I have in all?
- Is there a diet I should be on or that I should avoid? Vitamins? Drugs?
- Are there any activities I should avoid?
- What experiences have other patients had with chemotherapy?
- What is the possibility of sterility or birth defects in children?
- Do you recommend a port-a-cath into a bigger vein?
- When do we begin?
- Can I try using a diet program with the chemotherapy?

IMPORTANT INFORMATION TO KEEP

- Ask the doctor where your medical records are kept and how to access them if you want them.
- Keep your own health chart or summary of your experiences and vitals such as your weight, temperature, new aches and pains, heart rate, skin color, eyelid color, diet, frequency of going to the bathroom, sleep schedule, etc.

- Keep a journal. You will not recognize the significance of how you change until after chemo. You do not have to write much. Just a thought for the day or description of how you feel is sufficient.

OUTLINE FOR UNDERSTANDING PRAYER

The following outline will help you understand the relationship of the topics I discuss in this book and in my second book titled *PRAY: How God Answers Every Prayer*. It also shows that there are more topics to learn about than are covered in the book. If you would like to continue learning more about prayer, please visit patrickbriney.com.

THE PURPOSE OF PRAYER (CPR)

- Communion
- Praise
- Requests

FOUR FOUNDATIONAL TRUTHS OF PRAYER

1. God is in control at all times.
2. God hears every prayer.
3. God answers every prayer.
4. God's answers are always the best answers.

CRITERIA FOR PRAYERS TO BE GRANTED

- God's will for saving the maximum number of souls
- Minimum requirements: faith, belief, righteousness
- Extra mile prayers: persistence and fasting

THE FOUR TYPES OF PRAYER

1. Prayers for revelation
2. Prayers for desire
3. Prayers because of revelation
4. Prayers because God answers

ANSWERS TO PRAYERS

1. God answers every prayer.
2. Answers depend on the type of prayer offered.
3. Definitive answers include yes, no, or conditional requirements.
4. Silent answers indicate that the decision is yours or that you should wait on God.

GLOSSARY

Accept: To believe; consent as right.

Baptism: Though there are several baptisms such as of the Holy Spirit, of fire, unto Moses in the river, in Christ, etc., most commonly it is thought of as immersion into water as a work of obedience to God in order to qualify for membership in a local church.

Believe: Accepting that God is right.

Believer: One who accepts God's Word as true.

Body: The physical body.

Born again: Born again of God spiritually, thereby having God's righteous nature imputed to one's spirit.

Call: As in Romans 10:13, "For whosoever shall call upon the name of the Lord shall be saved." This means to have the perspective of depending on God.

Carnal: Inclination and perspective of indulging in sinful passions of the physical body rather than delighting in God.

Christ: The second person of the triune godhead known as Jehovah; also known as the anointed One of God, who is God manifested in the flesh (First Timothy 3:16).

Christian: One who is saved by Jesus Christ.

Church: Local assembly of believers who covenant with one another to do God's work God's way.

Communion: Fellowship and close relationship with God.

Confess: As in Romans 10:9, "That if thou shalt confess with thy mouth the Lord Jesus, and shalt believe in thine heart that God hath raised him from the dead, thou shalt be saved." Admission to God that He is right.

Faith: Revelation from God; the substance of things hoped for and evidence of things not seen.

Father: The first person of the triune Godhead known as Jehovah.

Flesh: The physical body, as in carnal.

God: Jehovah; the trinity of Father, Son, and Holy Spirit. Three persons (trinity), yet each being infinitely equal and indistinguishably one in nature, wisdom, power, purpose, and conclusions.

Grace: Favor from God that is undeserved; also referred to as unmerited favor.

Heaven: The dwelling of God where there is no sin.

Holy Spirit: The third person of the triune Godhead known as Jehovah.

Hope: Optimistic expectation especially of the immutable and guaranteed promises of God.

Inward man: The spirit and soul.

Jesus: The second person of the triune Godhead known as Jehovah.

Life: Spiritual life is defined by First John 5:12 as a relationship with Jesus Christ. Eternal life is a never-ending relationship with Jesus Christ.

Lord: A title given to God as the Lord of lords because He is the highest authority in creation.

Mercy: Not requiring that you pay for your crime or receive what you deserve.

Nature: As in the nature of man. It is the innate quality of what you are that determines your tendency and inclination. A sin nature is inclined to do things differently than what God would do. God's nature is the standard of righteousness. (See righteousness and unrighteousness)

New heaven and earth: The replacement creation after the current heaven and earth are melted down and obliterated.

Outward man: The physical body.

Praise: An expression of honor to God.

Prayer because God Answers: Prayer in response to God answering a request.

Prayer because of Revelation: Prayer that is offered because God told one to pray for something.

Prayer for personal desire: Prayer for something one wants.

Prayer for Revelation: Prayer request for God to reveal something such as an idea or guidance for making a decision.

Prayer: Talking to God that involves communion, praises to God, and requests of God.

Repentance: Change of mind and belief.

Request: A question asked of God.

Righteousness: The nature of God that can be given to others through new birth; also known as the born-again experience.

Salvation: God's deliverance of one who believes in Him, His forgiveness of sins, and the miraculous change of one's unrighteous nature to righteousness.

Sanctification: The work of God to make one righteous; the work of a believer to live right for God.

Sin: Anything contrary to God in nature, motive, or deed.

Soul: The conscience and identity of self.

Spirit: The spirit of man which is inseparable from the soul and enables the soul to interact with the spiritual world. (Also, see Holy Spirit)

Spirit-filled: To be under the control and influence of God.

Trust: Rely fully on God; totally dependent on Him.

Unbeliever: One who doubts or rejects God's doctrines and values as being true.

Unrighteousness: The nature of man or angels that is capable of tendencies (motive and behavior) that God would not approve of and is personally incapable of.

Works: Efforts on the part of people to impress God in order to deserve or earn the right to God's blessings. Works are anything a lost person (unbeliever) can do and often involve conforming to the Law of God.

THE AUTHOR

Dr. Patrick Briney is an author, speaker, and Bible teacher for practical Christianity serving as the senior associate pastor at Mission Boulevard Baptist Church in Fayetteville, Arkansas. He is a missionary to the University of Arkansas, the Founder and President of Leadership Training Institute of America, and the Founder and President of Life Changing Scriptures.

A scientist and former atheist turned Bible believer, Dr. Briney shares from the Bible and from God's designs in creation practical ways to live better, pray better, think better, and lead better.

As a student in 1974 at the University of California at Irvine, Pat was deeply committed to scientific reasoning. In his search to know if God exists, he was confronted with empirical evidence and sound reasons that it was more reasonable scientifically to believe that God did exist than that He did not. He could not deny the possibility of God.

God completed Pat's search with personal, divine confirmation by faith. Pat believed and accepted Jesus Christ as his Lord and Savior.

Not long after, the Lord impressed on Pat the importance of practical, relevant Christianity described in First Corinthians 10:31. He committed everything he did to glorify God, from family to education to ministry. After Pat transferred to the University of Arkansas at Fayetteville, the Lord added him to Mission Boulevard Baptist Church (MBBC) where he continues to teach others the practical, common-sense Christian values, doctrines, and life solutions that make Christianity relevant in today's culture.

While ministering on campus, Pat earned a Ph.D. in microbiology from the University of Arkansas, specializing in immunology and infectious diseases. During that time, he founded the Creation Science Society at the University of Arkansas and produced the Creation Insights seminars. He is regularly invited to conduct seminars on science and faith, as well as creation and evolution, and has debated atheists and evolutionists.

At MBBC, Pat served as outreach director and conducted evangelism campaigns into the community and on college campuses. As the discipleship director, he developed training materials and oversaw the annual MBBC discipleship conference. In 1996, Pat founded the Leadership Training Institute of America (LTIA), where he continues to train leaders to defend and live a Biblical worldview.

Dr. Briney doesn't just talk about being a Christian, he experiences it. When he asked God to teach him about the prayers that move mountains spoken of by Jesus in Mark 11:22–23, God gave him a mountain. Through the experience of stage 4B Hodgkin's lymphoma and its reoccurrence five years later, God granted Dr. Briney's prayer to understand prayer. That was over thirty years ago. He shares his experience and prayer lessons in his two books *HOPE: Lessons from a Cancer Survivor's Journey with God* and *PRAY: How God Answers Every Prayer*.

Pat and his wife, Colleen, live in Fayetteville, Arkansas. They have two grown daughters, a son-in-law, and two very energetic grandsons.

Made in the USA
Coppell, TX
17 December 2020